Principles
and Procedures
of Tour
Management

Principles and Procedures of Tour Management

PATRICK J.T. CURRAN

Foreword by
SAMUEL I. PORRATH

CBI

CBI PUBLISHING COMPANY, INC.
51 Sleeper Street, Boston, Massachusetts 02116

Library of Congress Cataloging in Publication Data

Curran, Patrick J T 1931–
    Principles and procedures of tour management.

    1. Tour guides (Persons).   I. Title.
G154.7.C87   658'.91'91   77–16399
ISBN 0–8436–0754–8

Printed in the United States of America

Contents

Acknowledgments

A work of this kind cannot be written without the kind cooperation of many capable people. The initial idea and encouragement to undertake the writing of this book was advanced by Dr. Samuel I. Porrath, the founder and Chairman of the Institute of Transportation, Travel and Tourism (TTT), at Niagara University. He was the first to point out to me the need for textual material dealing with escorts and tour managers, authored by experienced practitioners in the field, for use by schools offering courses in travel and tourism and by companies operating escorted tours. He also prepared the way for this publication. His sentiments were favorably augmented by Professor Willard Ellis of McGill University.

Dr. Porrath and the entire staff of the Institute of TTT, especially Mr. Howard Sellinger, made me feel welcome and put their valuable resources at my disposal. Many of the original chapters were used, reviewed, and tested in their classrooms, thus allowing them to give me their academic and practical points of view.

I am also deeply indebted to Ms. Amelia Schwartz of *Travel Weekly*, who opened the extensive library of that publication to my use; it was most helpful.

Others who supplied me with information and thoughts were

Mr. Lauin Martin of Greyhound, Ms. Marilyn Cooper of Four Winds Travel, Mr. Aldo Rinalde of American Express, Mr. Tom Mulroy and the staff of Faith Travel, Mr. Michael Billig of *Travel Trade,* Mr. Richard Kahn of *Travel Agent* Magazine, Ms. H. Kinsella of the faculty of the Institute of TTT and Gopack Travel & Tours, Inc., Mrs. Denise Slovberg of Canadian National Railways, Ms. Noreen Cartwright of Canadian Pacific Rail, Mr. Murray Vidockler of All State Bus Corp., Mr. Victor Geller of Geller-Howard Travel, Ltd., and the entire staff of the Canadian Government Office of Tourism.

On the production side, I gratefully acknowledge those who encouraged this undertaking and helped bring it to its fruition: first, Eileen Gallagher-Curran of Rockville Centre, N.Y. for taking my notes and typing the first drafts; Rev. Anthony Dittrich of Jasper, Alberta for his prayers and solicitude; Mr. & Mrs. Arthur Bianchi of West Hempstead, N.Y. and Ms. Virginia L. Stiles of Athabasca, Alberta for reading and commenting on the drafts; with particular gratitude, Mrs. Jannie LaRoe and Mrs. Josephine Lapointe of the Institute of TTT at Niagara University for preparing the final draft and being very helpful in many other ways; finally, the production staff of CBI.

List of Illustrations

The Role of the Professionals

BY SAMUEL I. PORRATH

Today, the very word *travel* evokes pleasure, glamour, and excitement.

It was not always so.

The word *travel* was developed from *travail,* meaning hardship, trouble, and danger.

Travel, indeed, for countless centuries was considered a perilous undertaking. Highway robbers, roadside thieves, pirates, and other evil elements awaited the traveler, to do him harm, steal his possessions, and often commit murder. Uncomfortable modes of transportation and crude, sparse, and improper accommodations added to the traveler's woes. While much of the inconvenience of travel stemmed from the primitive conditions and the hazards of nature, the worst problems were caused by human barbarism. A traveler was an easy mark for robbery, assault, or murder, a victim of the greed of organized bands of prowling bandits.

Traveling in bygone days entailed many difficulties. The unpredictable perils that were faced as desolate territory was traversed made voyaging the domain of only the adventurous souls. People congregated in order to travel in groups, in caravans, engaging armed sharpshooters as their guides. Today people also travel in groups, but for social and economic reasons. We look upon travel today as a delightful experience, for we can anticipate a smooth and pleasant trip.

Travel has come a long road.

Because of the frightening experiences encountered by people on the road, most religious faiths have incorporated in their services special prayers for the safety of travelers. The Hebrew book of liturgies contains a prayer that specifically describes the problems of the voyager. It is called "Prayer of the Road" and is recited at the beginning of a journey:

> "I implore you, my God, that you lead me in the ways of peace; that my steps be directed in peace and that I will reach my destination in peace. Deliver me from the attacks of any enemy; save me from the horrors of ambush and the pains of robbers and all those elements that create accidents and cause trouble by the wayside. Save me from all sorts of hurts and afflictions that bring ill to the world."

There is also a prayer of thanksgiving for the traveler to read upon his safe return, particularly if his excursion included crossing the oceans. The prayer is recited in the presence of a worshiping congregation, in front of the sacred Torah scrolls at the synagogue, and expresses gratitude for God's mercy in saving the traveler from evil forces. To the early scholars and teachers, a trouble-free trip was much the same as a successful and complete recovery from a severe illness.

Even though Saint Christopher, the patron saint of travel, has been demoted, Catholics and even many non-Catholics all over the world still use his medals as good luck charms to fend off evil forces and protect the traveler.

Today, too, we may encounter unpleasant or disastrous experiences in our travels. Airplanes may be hijacked. Unfortunate travelers may find themselves stranded, without accommodations or means to return home, despite the fact that they have paid dearly for these services. We often hear of unscrupulous price gouging, inadequate services, and gross mishandling, needlessly endured and suffered by travelers. Travel still has in it the element of travail. Uncommon as these bitter disappointments are, they nevertheless occur and affect many individuals and groups. Travelers still encounter dishonesty and misrepresentation, and their experiences make the prospect of traveling unattractive for many people.

In general, however, travelers enjoy pleasant experiences these days and look upon their tours, cruises, and trips—whether by land, air, or water—as interesting, stimulating, and rewarding undertakings. The general overall impression is excellent. Travel is delightful. Properly prepared for, it can provide all the comforts of home and more.

Travel has become a big business. In recent years, the U.S. travel industry has grown at a faster rate than most other sectors of the economy. The U.S. Travel Data Center reported that Americans spent over $75 billion while traveling to U.S. destinations a hundred miles or more away from home in 1975. The U.S. Department of Commerce reports that this does not include traveling overseas.

Travel methods have brought the farthest sections of the world within reach of all of us. It is a shrinking world in distance, yet still as spacious as ever and even more exciting. We get there faster, and we can enjoy being there more. We find it easier to make arrangements to get where we want to go—all thanks to the professionalism of a great industry called Travel and Tourism and to the great efforts invested by the people who manage the elements of transportation, travel and tourism, and the hospitality services. The talent and ingenuity of these men and women have created a new world of pleasure and brought rich rewards to today's traveler. They have mastered the art of providing comfort and assuring satisfaction and have professionalized this gigantic industry, fully compensating the clients in grand manner. When a tourist has reason for complaint, it is usually because he has entrusted the arrangements to amateurs, inexperienced and unprofessional personnel.

A traveler has many persons working for him. Some he will have contact with, and some he will never see. They are eager to serve him. The invisible workers are no less important to him than those he meets in person. When a traveler is careful and lucky, all of these workers will be professionals who understand his needs and will come to his aid efficiently, economically, and promptly. These are people who have learned the skills of their profession and have trained fully for their careers. They are proud of their work and approach it with dignity and authority. Travelers are willing to pay for the services that create a successful trip, and they are entitled to receive them. It does not cost more to engage a professional. Often, doing so results in great savings in time and funds and eliminates unnecessary aggravation.

Every traveler is a tourist if he is away from his home for a length of time, whether for pleasure, business, or health. While en route, or when stationed in the new environment, he needs a variety of services which, in turn, are provided by many agencies or individuals.

Travelers who want their affairs attended to with a minimum of trouble should patronize the professionals, the experts who are supposed to know how to handle any problems. When the traveler solicits the help of the expert, he eliminates the many entangling details involved in preparing for his journey. A traveler must buy transportation, but first he must ascertain the best route, carrier, or mode of transport. He must arrange for food and lodging and see that his baggage is taken care of. All of these arrangements must be methodically planned, coordinated and set up in advance. Any such arrangements that are related to the total needs of the traveler are called services. Some may be spartan, others luxurious. They fluctuate with the prices paid and with their availability. The tastes and pocketbook of the traveler dictate the extent and variety of the services demanded and furnished.

The people involved in the direct process of making these services available are the travel agent, the tourism expert, the hospitality manager, and the tour manager. These four work together. They must work together to be successful. As a unit, they must coordinate their services closely and meticulously. They complement and help each other as they arrange for the smooth operation of this great industry we call Travel and Tourism. Each takes over where another has left off. The take-over entails many minute details and requires efficiency and craftsmanship—the result of know-how.

The travel and tourism industry has mushroomed tremendously in the last few decades and is still developing at a fantastic rate. It has become an important factor in the economy of many nations, and some countries depend almost entirely upon this industry. Thousands of vendors deal with the travel agents and tourism experts and are wholly dependent upon them for their livelihood.

It would seem that there is not much difference between *tourism* and *travel* as professions and as businesses. We usually employ both terms as synonymous and interchange them in our daily speech. We assign to them, in our vernacular and daily references, similar properties and identical definitions. We attribute to travel agents and tourism experts similar qualifications, talents, and training. That is so because we do not fully understand the separate roles that each one plays. In today's specialized world, when professionalism and expertise are demanded, no matter what the career, it is important that we learn to appreciate the variations and the similarities. There is definitely a distinction between the two. Each represents a different prospective and perspective.

The travel agent and the tourism expert seem to work in opposite directions and yet work together. Both deal with the same product; yet their objectives are somewhat different. They concentrate their efforts in different directions, which lead to the same goal. The product they both market is a *destination,* plus the *services* and *accommodations* attached thereto. For both, the objective is to make an attractive promise, a valid obligation to provide proper transportation and accommodations for the tourist.

The tourism expert addresses himself to prospective visitors to his locale and advises them to contact the travel agent for the execution of their plans. From the travel agent, the traveler obtains stipulations for services as represented by tickets and vouchers. The travel agent relies upon the tourism expert to see that these services are available to his clients, subject, of course, to normal conditions. The travel agent provides the bodies; the tourism expert provides the accommodations, the atmosphere, and the élan.

The promises made to the traveler are spelled out in the contract we call an itinerary and may vary from tour to tour. The more that is promised, the more the tour costs. The more nights away from home, the better the hotel, the higher the costs. The longer the sight-seeing tour, the higher the tariff. Each attraction has a price tag. The expenses mount as one goes up the ladder from budget to economy class to first class, deluxe, and personal, individual catering.

The vendors are represented by one or more, or all, of the four agencies aforementioned. They provide the obligations covenanted in the agreements. They spell out the promises, which in turn are marketed by the tour operators and tour coordinators and sold directly to the public through the travel agents. Along the way, many other parties become signatories, obligated to deliver the various items in the contract. Altogether, they create what a traveler might today call a tour package, the consolidated promises of various vendors of services and goods.

In the travel business, the tour package means something else. *Discover America Package Tour Handbook,* published by Discover America Travel Organization (DATO), Washington, D.C., defines a package tour as

> A salable travel product which offers, at an inclusive price, several or more travel elements which would otherwise be purchased separately by a traveller. A tour package can include, in varying degrees, any or all of the following components: lodging, sightseeing, attractions, meals, entertainment, car rental, transportation by air, motor coach, rail or even private car. Oftimes it includes special events and especially tailored receptions and visits. A package has a pre-determined inclusive price, number of features and period of time. However, it can offer additional optional elements which permit the purchaser to extend the length of the package or purchase added features.

For our purpose, we shall call any total trip that a traveler has engaged a tour package.

The travel agent may be called, or at least compared to, an exporter. He exports bodies, alive and with money, and earns his funds from the commissions he receives from transport companies, tour operators, and sight-seeing attractions, whose services he buys for his clients. He buys these services through a travel wholesaler, a travel coordinator, or directly from the suppliers. He is the go-between, the liaison between the vendor and the purchaser.

Here are the technical and legal definitions of an agent:

General Agent—one employed in his capacity as a professional man or master of an art or trade, or one to whom the principal confides his whole business or all transactions or functions of a designated class; or he is a person who is authorized by his principal to execute all deeds, sign all contracts or purchase all goods, required in a particular trade, business or employment.

Agent—one who is authorized by another to act for him. One entrusted with another's business.

One who represents and acts for another under the contract or relation of agency. A business representative whose function is to bring about, modify, affect performance or terminate contractual obligations between principal and third party.

One who undertakes some business or to manage some affair for another, by the authority as on account of the latter, and to render an account of it.

One who acts for, or in place of, another by authority from him; a substitute, a deputy appointed by principal with power to do the things which principal may do. One who deals not only with things, as does a servant, but with persons, using his own discretion as to means, and frequently enters into contractual relations between his principal and third party.

The wholesaler often is the banker who risks large sums of money speculating in the industry. He buys "futures"—and his commodity is travel and tourism. He gambles by reserving sizable blocks of rooms far in advance, contracting for meals, guaranteeing transportation. He hopes that in due season people will buy these services and accommodations from him at a profit. He invests money in ventures. The travel agent is his outlet and contact. The travel agent deals directly with individual or group travelers. Through the agents, the wholesaler is able to unload the various services he has purchased. It takes, sometimes, many agents to sell the full commitment made by a wholesaler.

The tourism expert, on the other hand, has another role entirely. The character of his profession demands that he concentrate on the business of bringing people into his community. He is a promoter; he is a planner. In contrast with the travel agent, he might be compared to an importer. His is the job of persuading potential tourists to come to his locale. How does he do it? He works with the local organizations, encouraging them to support his efforts and supply provisions for the traveler. It is his task to develop attractions and organize interesting enterprises, fairs, and programs that will make his city or place a magnet, drawing travelers to it. Sometimes these attractions are natural, like Niagara Falls or the Grand Canyon. Sometimes they need to be augmented by man-made attractions like museums, aquariums, and theatrical presentations. Often such attractions must be imported, in order to draw travelers to the community. The tourism expert does the research and makes the necessary suggestions; he initiates, plans, organizes, and promotes.

To develop new destinations or upgrade old ones, the travel agent needs the professional assistance of the tourism expert, who provides the tools for selling a destination to the clients and insures that services will be provided, once the tourist has arrived. Both sell promises, and each looks to the other to carry them out. The line of demarcation between them is not as obscure as it might appear on the surface. Each serves in a specialized capacity. Both trade with the wholesaler, who often brings the two together.

To sell the services he has developed, the tourism expert likewise seeks and needs, directly or indirectly, the cooperation of travel agents in various communities throughout the land. He depends upon them to create customers for the attractions he has encouraged. The travel agent can send him the tourists to fill the hotels and restaurants he represents. These two professionals must, by the nature of their business, work in concert in order to complement and strengthen each other's services and make their jobs a success. One without the other would find it difficult to accomplish much.

The travel or tour package, of which we spoke earlier, is composed of additional components, whose contributions are of inestimable value: The hospitality factor, which includes food and lodging; the transportation element, which includes the airline carriers, the automobiles, the buses, the steamships; the sight-seeing business, which is a business all by itself and in its own way is a composite of all the other segments of the industry.

And finally, there is another professional, who is perhaps the most significant factor in determining the success or failure of a tour. He is the mainstay of the industry, inasmuch as it is he who deals most closely and intimately with the clients. All the others have made preparatory steps and laid the groundwork, but it is his work that consummates the package.

This unsung hero is the subject of our discourse. He is the ultimate agent and purveyor of all these services. He deals directly with the tourist, assuring that the services contracted for are provided, the promises fulfilled, the clients satisfied. He is the escort or tour manager whom we commonly call the tour guide.

The tour manager is, indeed, a very important link in an industry that involves billions of dollars; millions of people; innumerable programs; thousands upon thousands of attractions both natural and man-made; untold numbers of shops, souvenir stores, bus companies, large and small hotels and restaurants; and a host of ancillary services.

What is tourism? In brief, what is the travel business? More important, what part does the tour manager play?

Let's explore . . .

Where did the word *tourism* originate?

Tour is a Hebrew word. It derives its meaning from the Hebrew term *torah*, which means learning, studying, search. Torah is the name we give to Jewish law—the book that defines the Jewish way of life.

Let me remind you of a Sunday school lesson.

In the wilderness of Sinai, Moses designated twelve men to penetrate the land of Canaan, Israel's future Promised Land, to study its assets and liabilities, its strengths and its weaknesses. The Hebrew Bible plainly states that these men where charged to "tour" the land. They were to research the country's resources, observe its natural beauty spots, and assess its productivity. We call these men spies, because of their mission. They found what they were looking for by posing as tourists.

> These are the names of the men that Moses sent to *tour* the land of Canaan and he said unto them; Get you up into the South, and go up into the mountains. See the land, what it is, and the people that dwell therein, whether they are strong or weak, whether they are few or many. See what the land is that they dwell in, whether it is good or bad; what cities they are that they dwell in, whether in camps or in strongholds. What the land is, whether it is fat or lean, whether there are trees therein or not. Be ye of good courage. Bring of the fruit of the land with you. . . . And they went up and *toured* the land." [Num. 33:16-21]

In three thousand years, the concept of *tourist* has changed little.

A *tour* still, indeed, represents an attempt by the traveler to discover something about a place he visits. Sometimes he wants to see for himself something he has heard about. Sometimes he wants to learn about business opportunities, job possibilities, health advantages, educational benefits, environmental assets, or recreational properties. There are a thousand and one reasons for becoming a tourist. A tourist is one who learns, studies, and searches for data of interest to him.

Upon arriving in a new place, a tourist spends money in a variety of ways. Principally he buys food, lodging, transportation, and entertainment. Communities are eager to attract these people, in order to enhance the local economy, and they work very diligently toward this end. They know that the longer a tourist stays in the community the more money he leaves there. It is a simple business matter—and very large sums of money are involved. This is a multibillion-dollar industry.

Each traveler-tourist wants to receive new impressions or strengthen those he has already acquired. He travels for enjoyment and satisfaction, and the sense of excitement and adventure he derives from his trip makes it fun.

Thus, it may be stated that tourism is traveling to a destination laden with fun in search of fun. This three-letter word is the key to successful marketing of traveling and touring. It is what the traveler expects. It is what the travel agent sells. It is what the tourism expert promises. It is what the tour manager must help to deliver.

What is fun? The definitions are as varied as the individuals traveling the width and breadth of the globe. Fun knows no limits and has no borders. To some, fun might be an opportunity to see old ruins, inspect ancient sights, study bygone ways of life, become familiar with ancient history. These people might find satisfaction in archaeological digs, museums, or libraries. Others consider it fun to visit new and exciting places of entertainment. They look for opera houses and theaters, dance halls and fashionable shops. Some people look for antiques; others want the very latest styles in furniture, china, silverware, clothing, instruments, photographic and electronic equipment.

There is great fun in discovering new facts. Most travelers expect a trip to broaden their horizons and actively seek out intellectual enrichment. Some consider it fun to just walk about and meet new people, to observe local customs and absorb local color. Others search for the new and exotic. For many, good food is synonymous with fun. The opportunity to participate actively in various sports is fun for many, while just as many people prefer watching these sports. Some travelers are interested in religious objects, churches, synagogues, mosques, and temples, others in secular universities, schools, and colleges. Some find their fun in being with others, some in being alone and making their own discoveries.

All these people find themselves traveling together, each hoping to uncover an opportunity to satisfy his or her own brand of fun. Some are better able than others to articulate what they are looking for, but they all hope that, somehow, the tour manager will help them find a way to satisfy their desires.

Talented, hard-working, well-meaning professionals have worked together to create the product we call a *destination*. They have organized all the minute details that make the "package" attractive and salable. They have invested much energy, money, and time in planning and developing the program, aided by the people who sell food and lodging and who deal in the many other services designed to tempt the traveler.

These people, whose livelihood depends upon good service, have made all the arrangements they felt were required, only to learn, too late, that their labors have been frustrated because at the most crucial juncture in the package an immature, inexperienced, and ignorant guide has spoiled everything. All the efforts that have gone into organizing the package have been a prologue to the trip itself. When the trip is a disappointment, all the time, energy, funds, and dreams have gone to waste.

This is a very real danger. The entire enterprise can fail if the man or woman guiding the clients is unable to deliver the promises spelled out in the expensive, three-color brochures.

These promises represent a pledge, a contract. The tourist industry must deliver what is promised in an expert, professional manner.

Certain countries have learned this lesson and are tightening their requirements for tour managers to assure high standards. Israel is a good example. People returning from a visit to that country speak glowingly of their excellent guides. Tourism in Israel has made tremendous gains, thanks to these ambassadors of good will.

We have heard many complaints about the manner in which certain guides in the U.S.A. and other countries have treated their guests. The tourist industry cannot afford to allow unprofessionals to act in this capacity. The time has come to seriously consider the matter of licensing tour managers. For its own preservation, the industry must be encouraged to train, develop, and, above all, recognize the tour manager as a professional person.

Toward this end, college-level courses have been developed to train men and women for the profession of tour management. As the representative of a great industry, the tour manager holds a position of trust. His job requires a broad liberal arts background and demands such skills as writing, researching, and public speaking. In addition he must have a knowledge of finance and bookkeeping and must understand the complexities of the tourism business. Providing this background is the objective of such institutions of higher learning as the Institute of Transportation, Travel, and Tourism (TTT) at Niagara University.

The final and most important phase of the tour package should never be put into the hands of unqualified, unprepared, and ill-equipped guides. The time has come for the industry to give the pivotal position of tour manager the attention and recognition it deserves.

The tour manager must do more than sell his company's image, tell stories, and keep the group happy. He must be honest in his dealings with both vendor and client and knowledgeable about many subjects. He must be more than a jovial extrovert with a glib tongue.

He must keep thousands of facts stored in his head and update his information as conditions change. Fallacious stories and outdated statements are repeated year after year by guides who never attempt to improve their monologues. Such people are mere entertainers and contribute nothing to their clients' desire for knowledge. These people are more interested in earning extra commissions by "steering" their clients to their favorite shops and restaurants than they are in providing service and value. Often the tour manager works in concert with the local company representative who condones and encourages these practices.

Of course, such practices are not condoned by the entire industry. The reputable tour operators who oversee their guides and enforce good management should be commended, for they will contribute most to the professionalism of the industry.

There is no doubt that a tour guide, tour manager, escort—whatever you may call him—is a teacher, inasmuch as he gives his clients information relevant to the places they visit. His clients assume he has researched the material and rely on him to be factual, knowledgeable, and trustworthy. This is as it should be. This is why he was hired.

In the eyes of the clients, the guide is the expert on the tour, whether or not he has the proper background. Whatever he tells them will be disseminated widely. Like his counterpart, the teacher, the escort must therefore prepare his material with care and exactitude. The agency that engages him must carefully review his credentials, his knowledge, and his ability to act as an authority on the many subjects he may be called upon to discuss.

In the course of performing his duties, a guide may be asked for explanations when showing paintings; when pointing to archaeological discoveries; when narrating historical data; when chatting about local politics and discussing social values; when presenting material relating to schools and universities; when answering questions about ethnic matters; when advising about shopping or other entertainment; when talking about local cultural achievements and institutions. A guide is confronted with a thousand and one subjects in the course of his tours, as he delivers his "spiels" and calls attention to sights worth seeing.

And there are countless questions. A tour manager is bombarded with questions. His replies are considered authoritative and will be quoted. His clients assume that he has been placed in his responsible role because he has the necessary training. He should not be afraid to say, "Let me look it up for you." Condensed informational manuals are available for such occasions, and the tour manager should have a supply of them on hand. Sometimes, a simple inquiry at the local library, governmental or tourist office, or Chamber of Commerce will produce the answer.

The tour manager need not fabricate stories to add color to his narrations. With legitimate facts at his disposal, he should be able to make the truth as fascinating as any fiction he might create. Too many falsehoods are delivered as truths because guide after guide perpetuates these deceptions. Lying is unprofessional.

Besides being a guide, what function does the professional tour manager serve?

Properly prepared for his profession, the tour manager can, if given the opportunity, provide tremendous assistance to the travel and tourism industry. Unfortunately, he has been relegated to nursing clients and keeping them happy. The industry has not fully availed itself of his potential input.

The planners, the programmers, and the marketing people would do well to invite the guide to sit in with them as they develop their routes, programs, and attractions and plan for lodging, food, and extras. Who is better informed than the tour manager on the performance of the hotel people, the restaurants, the attractions, and, in general, on the efficacy and value of the items in the itinerary? Tour operators, unfortunately, seldom solicit their managers' advice. The fact that there is no close coordination between the managers and the tour companies in the preparation, development, and revision of tours is a source of concern to many tour managers. They are eager to help, but their talents have not been fully utilized.

Most large tour companies are organized into a number of divisions. Tour managers come under the operations division, while tour planning is a division in itself. Planning receives reports from the escorts only if they are negative and call for some form of action. Otherwise, the escorts' daily reports are never seen by the planning department. This is where the tour industry fails to take advantage of its own resources. The well-trained tour manager should be recognized as a professional, and recognition should begin with the industry itself.

The professional tour manager could become an important member of the planning team. His recommendations and counsel in designing a tour could be valuable, for he speaks from experience and knows who renders acceptable services and who does not. The ideas proposed by an experienced tour manager could be of significant help in planning, preparing, developing, and revising a tour. But his expertise generally is not used, nor is his advice sought by the industry.

Here is the way one old-timer in the business, a tour manager of long standing, puts it.

> Most large tour operators are broken down into divisions. The Tour Manager comes under the Operations division while tour Planning is under a Planning division. The daily escort reports are sent over for some type of action. This is, for the most part, the extent of the manager's input.
>
> One large tour company has two Managers that it keeps on the payroll year round. When not on tours both men are used by the sales department, visiting agents and travel shows. Both of the managers and the operations department have repeatedly asked to have them assigned to planning so that they may offer aid and expertise where most needed. Their pleas are ignored.
>
> Since most tour managers are "independent contractors" their costs

(salaries, etc.) are included in the expense budget of Operations. The tour operators consequently have no budget for Tour Managers to be utilized in any other division. This is unfortunate.

The fact, however, is that the Tour Managers are constantly in the field of operation. They are aware of new hotels, restaurants and attractions. They are also the ones who come face to face with the problems of particular facilities. The tour operators should be made to realize that they have a gold mine of information at their disposal which they are not tapping. My advice is: "begin to use it."

This does not mean that they would have to employ the managers on a full time basis. A one or two day period of meeting with the planning department, going over the tours that he has worked that season would be a good start. It could begin with "If you could redesign the tour, what changes would you make?"

Another contribution that the tour managers can make is by visiting the hotels and other suppliers during the "off season" and going over the problems that had occurred during the high season. "Why is it that tour company A always gets the best rooms while company B gets the rooms overlooking the parking lot and the kitchen?"

This is very hard to do when a tour checks into a hotel at 4:30 and leaves the next morning and the person in charge of the hotel has already left for the day.

We Tour Managers are saying to the companies; you trust us with your clients, your money, and when there are problems, you call on us and we help you out of them. Now, let us help you further in planning, not only to improve your tours and increase your sales but also to help you avoid recurring problems.

All in all, we have in the tour manager a very important person. When we all recognize the valuable service he performs and help him to become more proficient and more professional, the travel and tourism industry will reap the benefit of higher profits and greater efficiency.

This handbook has been composed as an initial step in providing the aspiring tour manager with a guide, as he learns the professional aspects of the tourist business.

Dr. Curran, has, in my opinion, created a very valuable document worthy of wide dissemination among present and future members of this important, pivotal, and honorable profession.

Samuel I. Porrath
Chairman,
Institute of Transportation, Travel and Tourism
Niagara University

March 1978

PART 1

The Concept of Tour Management

*I will send you to Pharaoh
to lead my people, the
Children of Israel, out of
Egypt.*
Exod. 3:10

1. A NEW PROFESSION FROM AN AGE-OLD CONCEPT

If a word association test included the use of the term *guided tours,* the most common reply would probably be "Cook's." Why Cook's? Because, in the modern sense of the word, Thomas Cook was the father of supervised touring, and his name has become synonymous with guided tours.

Cook organized his first guided tour in 1841. Four years later, he became a full-time excursion organizer.[1] History, however, records that centuries before that, as early as 1085, Pope Urban II issued the call, "Deus lo volt" (God wills it), and launched a series of expeditions that were to become known as the Crusades. While the pope was responsible for starting the Crusaders on their way, it was the Venetians who arranged the physical transportation to the Holy Land.[2] Going back still further in history, we can find a complete record of what was probably the first escorted tour with all of its problems. It was an expedition of unusual events and circumstances, and the tour manager was called upon to work miracles. When he could not get ships to cross the Red Sea, he had to literally part the waters, making it possible for the more than half a million souls to arrive on the other side. He had to work another miracle to provide food for his people in the wilderness of Sinai. It took him forty years to travel a distance that could have been covered in a dozen days or two weeks.

The tour manager of today, while not facing the monumental problems of Moses, does not have the easy job that the public, or even his own family, seems to think he has. Those not familiar with the profession often picture the tour manager as visiting exotic places, lodging in the finest hotels, eating gourmet foods, and meeting interesting people. Some company has made all of the arrangements in advance, they believe, so all the escort has to do is ride along and check people into hotels. A tour manager's job would be utopian if this indeed were true. Don Short, in his book on travel careers, gave a very honest appraisal of the tour manager's job when he said:

It is one thing to meet a tour director at a social event and chat eruditely about the faraway places with strange sounding names that he visited. It is quite another thing to watch him at work in some far distant port when a local hotel clerk has mislaid all the passports for his touring group, a nice old lady from Dubuque has had an asthma attack, and the absent minded professor from New Haven can't find his glasses and, therefore, has to have all the menus and sightseeing schedules read to him. No one works harder than the traveling worker in the travel industry. You have to have a special kind of love for the adventure and excitement of being in distant places, dealing with a varied assortment of humanity, and combining the talents of a psychologist, teacher, nurse and social counselor.[3]

All this hard work and expenditure of talent will bring rewards found in few other careers. It is without a doubt a glamourous job. In many ways it is a job to be envied. A tour manager goes to exciting places, eats in the finest restaurants, enjoys excellent entertainment, stays at famous hotels, and, most important, gets paid for it. To the groups he leads, he really is a Moses, who performs miracles and executes the seemingly impossible. His clients will seek and accept his advice on all sorts of matters, even very personal ones. When the tour is over, some of his clients may become close friends, and others will remember him with holiday cards ten years later.

Tour management can also be financially rewarding. While the base salaries in the profession are low, they are, for the most part, potential savings as the manager also receives a daily subsistence for meals, laundry, and other expenses, which should, with proper management, cover all personal expenses while on tour. One must also include, as part of the financial compensations of the job, tips, group overrides, special discounts. These are, for the most part, good fringe benefits which serve to offset the low base pay. Compensation will be discussed in Part V. All of these things combine to make tour management a lucrative and highly satisfying profession.

Throughout this book, the title "tour manager" will be used. This term refers to a person with advanced training and education who has demonstrated his or her ability to research and prepare a tour, to guide it and explain it, and to make it an unusual and memorable experience; who has the necessary pleasing personality, traits, and common sense to conduct a tour successfully; and who thus meets the requirements for membership in the International Association of Tour Managers. Historically, the term used for people who guided group tours was *escort* in North America and *courier* in Europe. The title *guide* was, and still is, used only for someone employed to lead local sight-seeing at a particular place or city. Following the Second World War, when expansion of air travel brought touring within the means and reach of the middle classes, many persons were employed as tour leaders. Unfortunately, many of them had only limited or, in some cases, no training in this sensitive field. The result was a growing dissatisfaction on the part of tour operators and clients with the poor caliber of practicing escorts. One reason why the International Association of Tour Managers was formed was to protect the public and prevent this important profession and growing industry from being prostituted and mishandled. Robert McMullen, a president of the American Society of Travel Agents, has called for a professional training program for tour leaders that would "create a pool of qualified individuals which would be drawn upon by a tour operator, travel agency, or visitor."[4] He added that "We [the United States] are the most undeveloped country for tourism going."[5]

This book was written to meet this need. It is the result of seventeen years of experience in the field of tour management. The procedures and forms outlined in the book are representative of those used by all tour operators.

Tours are people, and just as no two people are exactly alike, neither are two tours. No matter how much education and experience one has, one will always run into new situations requiring new insight and fresh approaches. A good manager always keeps in mind Murphy's Law: "If anything can go wrong, it will."[6] One must expect the unexpected. One must be able to adjust to rapidly changing situations and learn to live out of a suitcase for long periods of time. If married, one must have a very understanding spouse. Dealing with human beings with their diverse personalities requires alertness, understanding, and the ability to adapt to constantly changing situations and climates. Tour management requires all the commitments of any profession, beginning with good education and proper training. While it is, in part, a glamourous job, it entails much hard work. Properly executed, it is emotionally and financially rewarding. We who are in the profession are proud and happy and look forward to greater rewards and recognition. Touring with escorts is developing into a major industry. The growing professionalization of this segment of the tour business has aroused the interest of educators and business leaders as well as government bodies.

QUESTIONS FOR DISCUSSION

1. How does the public concept of the tour manager's job compare with the actual situation?
2. What are the major financial rewards of the profession of tour management?
3. What are the major nonfinancial rewards offered in this profession?
4. Why are no two tours exactly alike?

NOTES

1. Donald Lundberg, *The Tourist Business,* 3rd ed. (Boston: CBI Publishing Company, Inc., 1972), p. 104
2. For a more complete history of travel, see: A.J. Burkart and S. Medlik, *Tourism* (London: Heinemann, 1974), and "A Short History of Tourism," *Travel and Tourism Encyclopedia* (London: Travel World, 1959).
3. Donald Short, *Opportunities in Travel Careers,* Vocational Guidance Manuals (New York: University Publishing and Distributing Corp., 1966), p. vi.
4. *Travel Weekly,* Nov. 28, 1974, p. 1.
5. Ibid., p. 51.
6. *Time,* Dec. 8, 1975, p. 36.

PART 2

The Profession of Tour Management

Profession: 1. A vocation requiring knowledge of some department of learning. . . . 2. The body of people engaged in an occupation or calling to be respected by the profession.
The American Family Dictionary

2. QUALIFICATIONS

As a tour manager, you are a professional in the full sense of the word. Like a practitioner of law, medicine, dentistry, or any other profession, you must acquire the necessary educational background and training to carry out your duties if you are to succeed. For the most part, you are an independent contractor. When you are working, you will be on call twenty-four hours a day. You will encounter no two situations exactly alike. Your education will never be complete. You will be reading and upgrading your knowledge constantly. You will also be using a vocabulary distinctive to the travel industry. All this is what makes the operation of this business such an exciting adventure.

Education and Training

Most professions have moved toward professional certification of members based upon successful completion of advanced educational requirements, usually a graduate degree with broad liberal arts or sciences undergraduate preparatory education. Until quite recently, the only training in the field of travel, transportation, and tourism was acquired on the job, and not all the training was valid. Training is only as good as the teachers.

In the past decade, however, a number of schools have been founded to train people for the industry. A 1974 survey of schools offering such training courses found that as a group "the commercial career schools and vocational colleges have the most uneven reputation in the trade."[1] Correspondence courses did not fare well either, except for one offered by the American Society of Travel Agents (ASTA), which is open only to employees of ASTA member agencies. Noncredit courses (many offered by universities) drew slightly higher ratings. The four-year, accredited colleges and universities, however, earned the highest ratings and have the best reputation. The survey listed thirteen institutions of higher learning offering courses in the broad field of travel and stated that there were others.[2]

Niagara University, at Niagara Falls, N.Y., in 1968 established the Institute of Transportation, Travel, and Tourism (TTT) under the leadership of its founder, Dr. Samuel I. Porrath. The Institute grants a baccalaureate degree in TTT. Other institutions offer a B.B.A. with a specialty in the field to their graduates. McGill University was the first to offer a graduate program with a diploma in management, tourism; or an M.B.A. in tourism. The University of Hawaii also offers a graduate program. Other universities, such as the New School of Social Research, have begun graduate programs in TTT or have them in the planning stage.

The industry has been pleased with this growing professionalism and indeed has encouraged its growth. Howard Apter, writing in *The Travel Agent,* points out that today "on-the-job training is a very dangerous thing especially if such people are allowed to handle clients."[3] There is, he says, an urgent need for a neophyte to obtain an overview "before he or she can grasp what today's travel business is all about. And such an overview can only be obtained from well structured university courses."[4]

For persons employed in the travel industry, the Institute of Certified Travel Agents in Wellesley, Mass., offers courses in the field. To those travel agents who pass the four required examinations and satisfactorily complete a research paper on an original topic, the ICTA grants the title Certified Travel Counselor. If the passing student is not a travel agent but is employed in the industry, the title granted is Certified Travel Associate. These courses are now being made available to people outside the industry.

In discussions with the author about the qualifications of a good tour manager, the executives of many tour companies pointed out that their most successful tour managers have broad backgrounds in the social sciences, particularly history, geography, and political science, and a good command of the English language. One must have the broad educational background necessary for an intelligent outlook and cultural appreciation. While in the past a command of one foreign language was considered essential, this ability has become less important in escorting English-speaking groups. The Europeans and Asians have done an excellent job of training their tourist-oriented personnel in the English language;

the second-language requirement, once basic, is becoming obsolete.

A good tour manager must also have training in methods of dealing with the varied situations that can and will arise while on tour. Most of these situations can be covered in a classroom setting and in textbooks, but as the Greyhound World Tours training manual stresses: "The most scholarly work, however, could not possibly cover all of the unusual situations with which you will be faced while carrying out your duties. The only basic *guide line* that we can give you for these unusual situations not covered by the enclosed instructions is *COMMON SENSE.*"[5]

The Manager's Personality

"I once knew a man who could speak fifteen languages but could not utter an original thought in any one of them" is an old saying. Education and training mean nothing unless you can communicate this expertise to your clients. Imparting knowledge is very important; indeed, the essence of a tour manager's job is communication. To be an effective communicator, you must possess the following traits.

Leadership—The company that contracts your services gives you the responsible task of leading its groups. Every group needs a good leader, and that leader is you. How good you are depends on how well you are prepared for the job. It is your responsibility to execute the plans and make the decisions. Your clients need to trust you and must be convinced that you are capable and responsible. You must establish your leadership in a positive and friendly way, not in a militaristic, autocratic, and arbitrary manner. People select escorted tours to avoid worries; they want to travel with a friendly group. If they note that you are always first on the scene, that you are calm, collected, and smiling, they will feel that they are in good hands. Keep your cool and stay happy at all times. Your clients will react with friendliness and cooperation. Comments such as, "I've called the hotel and they will be ready for us upon arrival," or, "I notified the restaurant that we will be half an hour late and they are changing their plans accordingly," are reassuring. They show that as a leader you are planning ahead and thinking of the members of the group under your care. But make sure you have really placed these calls before making such statements. Do not lie. The British psychologist, Dr. William McDougall, in his book, *The Group Mind,*[6] outlines ways of fusing individual minds into a group mind. His methods can be applied to tours. A group open to your leadership is more receptive to your suggestions and easier to control.

Tact—Every group starts as a collection of individuals with different personalities. As individuals, they have their likes and dislikes, their particular traits and tastes. Molding these individuals into a united group is your first on-the-road challenge. Escorted tours, in the past, tended to attract mainly mature people, many of whom were rigid in their outlook and had difficulties adjusting to new situations. In 1975, a Gallup poll of air travelers showed that "complete packages attract a small minority of travelers, mostly those who are inexperienced or older."[7] But one year later, a survey of motor coach tour operators showed that "there has been a change over the past year or so. . . . It's a result of the gas crunch and a slow economy. . . . There is still that hard-core senior market but now a younger market with more youths and families."[8] It is reasonable to assume this trend will continue. We will be faced with the energy crisis for a long time, encouraging group travel and discouraging expensive independent travel.

Interestingly, a 1976 study of motor coach tours by the Research Information Centre in Phoenix found that "The motor-coach tour customer is about the same in income level and social status as other [travel agency] customers although there is a slight skew toward the lower income."[9]

How do you reach the various people included in this diverse group? As tour manager, it will be necessary for you to be *tactful* in persuading the tourists to be cooperative with one another and tolerant of each other's demands and expectations. You must help them understand the importance of cooperating with you and with each other. Invite their attention, cooperation, and help with patience and understanding.

Patience and Understanding—As a manager, you will be a counselor, a finder of lost articles, a surrogate for a married son or daughter, at times even a parent figure. There is no limit to the roles you will play. Accept these roles naturally as part of your job. Usually, your clients need only a kind word or a smile. Be ready with such reassurance, even when you have heard the same story for the third, fourth, or fiftieth time. Patience is a virtue that rewards handsomely.

No matter how carefully you have done your job and how correctly you have made your reconfirmation calls, many hotels will not be fully ready when you arrive with your group. Buses may be late or break down. These are the times when your patience will be pushed to the edge. It is essential that you keep calm; otherwise, the morale of the entire group will disintegrate. If you can communicate your patience and understanding in such exasperating situations, the group will reciprocate with patience and understanding. They will respond to your emotional reactions, not your words. By reacting calmly yourself, you will learn to articulate your emotions and create an aura of serenity.

Sense of Humor—A sense of humor is a necessary personality trait for anyone who deals with the public. It will help you keep your sanity when all else fails. It will be a great asset to you and the group if you can relieve tension by pointing out the humorous side of some unexpected delay. There is humor inherent in everyday experiences on the tour, but you must ferret it out and expose it so that your clients can enjoy it. Of course, you must never make any individual, any ethnic or religious group, the butt of your humor. Your humor should be decent, clean, and devoid of any hurtfulness for anyone.

Firmness—In our profession, there are times when all other approaches fail and firmness is necessary—for example, when dealing with a client who is consistently late, thereby holding up the tour. Being firm does not mean being abusive. It simply means taking a stand for the benefit of the majority of the group. It means knowing what you intend to do and how to do it.

Appearance

Dress codes in schools and industries are a thing of the past, but in our profession they probably will never disappear. Proper dress is essential, as is good grooming. In general, your wardrobe should reflect the type of tour you are managing. The group's first impression of you is important in establishing your role as leader. Therefore, at the first meeting of the group, you should (if a man) wear a shirt with tie and jacket and (if a woman) a dress or pantsuit. Proper dress means good taste and understatement rather than flamboyant attire.

Ethics

Like any other professional, a tour manager has certain definite ethical responsibilities: (1) to the company that employs him, (2) to the providers of service to the tour, and (3) to the clients on the tour. You owe your employer your very best efforts in return for a fair wage. This means that your reports will be filed when due and that you will give honest appraisals of the hotels and other suppliers as called for. While you are working for a company, it is the only one you work for. The tour you are conducting should never be compared with those you conducted before or those of other companies. Disparaging remarks on your part are not only unfair to your employer but disappointing to your clients.

Speaking about the manager-company relationship, the International Association of Tour Managers states:

> You have been chosen by a responsible firm of Tour Operators to be the Tour Manager in charge of their clients, and *you too,* carry the responsibility for their product. All along the line, from the Tour Operator who planned the tour, designed an expensive brochure to sell it, and advertised it, to the Travel Agent who sat down in his office with the prospective buyer, doing booking details, [making] long distance telephone calls, writing air tickets for him, and turning him into a member of your tour group. Even your image has been part of the sales approach—"The Tour Manager [is the] epitome of skill and knowledge of the area, tact and diplomacy."

A vast amount of money has been spent on advertising and promotion, planning and operation, and you become the focal point, a fulcrum on which the whole tour swings—Success? or Failure? You are the critical link in the whole chain, from conception of the tour to the client's happy return home; but you are not the most important link—*All are important*; all have a part to play in bringing the client, prepared to travel with you. You must give full support and recognition to the preceding work, work done long before you appeared on the stage and you *must not disassociate yourself* from these preparatory operations, even if you feel there has been or is a weak point.

When your clients return home at the end of their tour, your conduct of the tour, and of yourself, will be preeminent in their minds when they talk to the person from whom they bought the tour. Be loyal to your firm, giving it your support in every way, because YOU are the representative of the firm, as well as being the Tour Manager, and your firm has entrusted you with its tour. You strengthen your own position as you protect and support your company's good name—It is quite simple, you are employed for that.

You will appreciate this more clearly, when after several seasons, successfully, with the same company, they will give you better tours, and your position will be strengthened with them.[10]

You must cooperate with the suppliers of services so they can execute their contracts with your employer as expeditiously as possible and complete them to your full satisfaction. Some may have problems occasionally, and a little assistance from you in explaining these problems to your clients will help assure a smoothly running tour. Be honest with your people and explain fully without creating animosity toward the suppliers. Difficulties will always arise; we are dealing with human beings, and mistakes will always happen. Obtain all of the facts before you act, and if the problem is unusual, report it as such. If, however, the supplier has a recurring problem that he seems unable or unwilling to correct, you must report this to your employer and take appropriate steps to remedy the situation for your group. People talk and compare notes, and unsatisfactory treatment will cause you loss of patronage on future trips.

It is to your clients that you owe the most. They are your bosses. You are fully responsible for their happiness and welfare.

You must concentrate all your attention on carrying out this responsibility with ease and competence. This is your prime duty. Very often, you will meet someone on a tour with whom you will develop a more than casual friendship, but this should never become apparent to the rest of the group. Similarly, do not allow one person or subgroup to monopolize your time. Be impartial, and give equal attention to all. Jealousy and envy, when allowed to fester, ruin a trip, and everyone suffers, you most of all.

Your purpose is to lead. Do not impose your moral standards or other values on any individual or group. Remember, you are a guide or escort, not an evangelist. Do not preach. "Live and let live" should be your motto, unless a client's or subgroup's behavior becomes distracting to other members of the tour. Even then, you must be sagacious and tactful so as not to create problems and raise sores that might become abrasive.

The profession of tour management demands education, training, leadership, and the ability to communicate. Expertise and knowledge are what the clients pay for, and they have a right to expect them. You will never know enough. You must update your education constantly; read more books, learn what is going on in the world of politics, commerce, sports, and entertainment. You must pay constant attention to your wardrobe and grooming, and in all situations you must be guided by a strong code of ethics and common sense.

3. TRAVEL AND TOURS

Why People Travel

It is only recently in the history of man that travel has been associated with pleasure. Previously, travel was always associated with hardship and trouble; the root word of *travel* is *travail* (suffering). The westward migration of pioneers across North America in the eighteenth century cannot be compared to a trip by auto today across the Trans-Canada Highway or Interstate 70.

Throughout history most travel was undertaken for economic reasons. Some traveled in order to find a new home, others traveled to escape from war, and so on. With the advent of modern transportation (railroads, steamships, the automobile, and commercial airlines), travel for pleasure became feasible, attractive, and within the reach of many people. This type of travel has grown remarkably in the twentieth century. A 1967 survey conducted by the U.S. Department of Commerce showed that only 16 percent of traveling engaged in by U.S. citizens was for business purposes, while almost 40 percent was for pleasure.[11] A 1970 survey showed that "pleasure travel accounted for seventy-five percent of international travel, and about fifty percent of domestic travel in this country [the U.S.]."[12] In 1976, a *New York Times* survey found that after a slight downturn during 1975 pleasure travel by American citizens was continuing to grow.[13]

John A. Thomas, in studying what motivates people to travel, isolated eighteen factors he considered significant:

1. To see how people in other countries live, work, and play
2. To see particular sights
3. To gain a better understanding of what goes on in the news
4. To attend special events
5. To get away from the everyday routine
6. To have a good time
7. To achieve some sort of sexual or romantic experience
8. To visit places your family came from
9. To visit places your family or friends have gone to

10. Weather (for instance, to avoid cold of winter or heat of summer)
11. Health
12. Sports
13. Economy (inexpensive living)
14. Adventure
15. One-upmanship
16. Conformity (keeping up with the Joneses)
17. To participate in history
18. Sociological motives (get to know the world)[14]

Prof. Donald E. Lundberg has developed sixteen reasons why people travel:

1. Business
2. Pleasure
3. Health
4. The need for a change
5. Rest and relaxation
6. To search for the exotic
7. To learn
8. To experience natural power, beauty, and wonder
9. Ego enhancement
10. For sports
11. To shop
12. Travel for travel's sake
13. To gamble
14. Travel as a challenge
15. For acceptance
16. For spiritual values[15]

Lundberg studied each of these reasons and pointed out that some may overlap on any particular trip.

It is difficult to say where business begins and pleasure ends when the business traveler is attending a convention in Las Vegas or Florida where as much as half of his time will be spent gambling or gamboling. The trip to Europe may involve contacting potential customers but it may involve sightseeing or an evening at the Folies Bergères. To further confuse the distinction, his wife may be along on a business trip.[16]

Health has been a prime reason for travel for many centuries. The spas and mineral baths of Europe drew great numbers of travelers in the eighteenth and nineteenth centuries. The warm springs of Banff led to its establishment as Canada's first national park. While spas have declined in popularity in this century, one U.S. president praised the rejuvenating effects of Warm Springs, Ga. Today, it is the sun, rather than hot sulfur water, that attracts the tourist. Many people travel to the desert or other sunny regions to take advantage of the sun's salubrious qualities. The sun moves people from one place to another in immense numbers as people from the cold north descend on Florida and the Caribbean at the height of winter. "Following the sun" is a major travel incentive for many. Others go where the snow is abundant and skiing is available.

Many young North Americans take the first real trip away from their homes and families when they are matriculated in a college located in another area. Travel for advanced education has become very popular and increasingly is being considered a must by many in the name of diversification and broadening of educational programs. Credit for travel has become an important segment of higher education programs. Conventions, seminars, and courses in a variety of subjects are interwoven with travel experiences. Foreign institutions all over the world are involved in travel programs. Thus global travel has become a very important part of higher education, particularly at the graduate level.

Professional organizations and international businesses often hold conventions in different parts of the country or even in different countries each year, exposing their members to various parts of the globe and offering wider exposure for the organizations. This practice has been adopted recently by some large companies for their annual stockholders' meeting. When people undertake a journey to attend a seminar, lecture, workshop, or other meeting, the journey itself becomes a learning situation, and this is as it should be. These experiences should combine pleasure and business, relaxation and work. Meetings held to exchange new ideas and present new techniques and products are proliferating, and provisions are usually made to include tours and side trips to interesting places.

The World Series, the Stanley Cup, the Super Bowl, and championship boxing matches have always attracted sports fans from faraway places to the cities where they are held. In recent years, agencies and hotels have begun to offer special golf and/or tennis packages and tours.

Some places—for example, Hong Kong—have advertised themselves as shopper's bargain spots. Who can resist a bargain even when it involves high air fares? This interest in bargains has led to group tours to shopping centers that offer "factory outlets" and "discount sales."

The introduction of OTC arrangements has made it possible for many people to enjoy a low-cost Las Vegas or Reno gambling weekend, and some cruise ships and Caribbean spots now enjoy the fame once held only by Monte Carlo. Gambling is apparently a great motivator of travel. Since cities and states see this as a stimulant to increased tourist business, we will doubtless see gambling casinos spring up in many communities.

People whose motive is ego enhancement believe they will derive a feeling of superiority or importance from their travels. A lower-middle-class North American traveling through the "third world" may feel that he is superior to the people he sees. On a more general level, to be waited upon in restaurants and to receive any number of services in a hotel (at the dial of a telephone or a snap of the fingers) give some people a feeling of importance difficult to experience at home. In addition, travel provides a topic of conversation and contributes to one's store of memories.

Travel for acceptance, according to Lundberg, is a motive often found among members of minority groups who may not feel completely comfortable in their home geographic area; they holiday in other areas where they feel more accepted. We all want to be recognized and to feel important.

The most potent reason for travel is the need for escape or change. "Escape from the dull, daily routine. Escape from the familiar, the commonplace, the ordinary. Escape from the job, the boss, the customers, the commuting, the house, the lawn, the leaky faucets."[17] As McCall and Havermann have pointed out, this need for a change from the daily routine is a basic human need. The human organism needs occasional change in order to operate optimally. "Basic nature seems to demand some kind of stimulation, and especially change in stimulation. The tendencies to seek out new sights to see, and new sounds to hear, are examples of stimulus needs."[18]

As our culture has moved away from the Puritan ethic of all work and no play, the public has readily accepted the need for change for change's sake. Leisure is no longer considered "sinful," and as the amount of disposable income has risen, travel has become an accepted way of finding efficacious changes in stimulation. We have learned to alter drastically our attitude toward leisure. No longer considered a luxury, it is, little by little, becoming for many a way of life. Periodic "getaways" are part of the routine of many.

The pilgrimage is one of the oldest reasons for travel known to man. The devout Muslim is required to make at least one trip to Mecca during his lifetime. Almost every quarter century, the pope declares a Holy Year during which many Catholics make a special effort to visit Rome. Jews the world over attempt to visit Israel and stand before the Western Wall, once known as the Wailing Wall, in Jerusalem. For years, the Franciscan Fathers have organized tours from New York City combining visits to religious shrines with the best of ordinary sight-seeing. Many other church groups or religious leaders organize similar journeys. These in truth are both pilgrimages and vacations. They satisfy a religious yearning, but provide an opportunity for great enjoyment.

Helen of Troy, according to legend, had a face that launched a thousand ships. The call of beauty, be it the *Mona Lisa*, the Rockies, or some exotic island, still beckons people from across the land and/or sea.

Finally, we have the adventurous soul who attempts to do the uncommon. *Time* magazine published a feature article on adventure vacations that are growing rapidly in popularity.[19] Many tourists to Mexico have heard old hands say that the only way to know Mexico is to take a "second-class bus," to mingle with the people and become acquainted with native folklore. In 1975, Allan Wilgus, of the AAA World Wide Travel, organized an "80

Hour around the World Tour."[20] Returning from this whirlwind tour, many passengers said that the trip was stimulating, a challenge they had been eager to be a part of. There is excitement in adventure; people like to be challenged. Each individual has, in fact, his own reason for visiting new places or old stamping grounds.

As a tour manager, it will be your responsibility to subtly ascertain your clients' motivation in taking this particular tour and then to see to it that these desires are fulfilled, if possible. The tour company packages dreams, the travel agent sells the dreams, but it is the tour manager who brings the dreams to fruition.

Why People Take Escorted Tours

It would be impossible to list all the reasons for choosing escorted tours over independent travel. However, some motives seem to be common to the bulk of guided-tour clients, although they may vary with each group or individual.

Companionship—The social nature of man provides an important reason for group travel. We all want to belong. We seek the company of other human beings when away from home. "Man, the social animal, feels comfortable in a group tour. He is with others of his kind who are predictable, a camaraderie develops; he is 'safe and secure from all alarm' as the hymn goes."[21]

The camaraderie of the individuals found on the great trains, on the steamships during their transoceanic journeys, and in the early days of air travel is now gone. Then, a person traveling alone could strike up a conversation with his table mates in the dining car and then adjourn to the parlor car or club car for further conversation. The bon voyage party, the captain's table, differentiation by class, and games galore made it easy for the individual or couple traveling alone on an ocean liner to meet "their kind of people" and quickly become part of a group. As air travel has lost its glamour status and become an ordinary means of transportation available to all, conversation between seatmates has diminished. This loss of group identity has forced the individual traveler who is seeking companionship to join a group tour.

Loneliness is abhorrent to people. Many consider it the curse of mankind. In a group, one may find compatible people; friendships develop that last for years and years; and much later the trip is relived with a note on a holiday card: "Remember the night we got lost in . . . " or, "Do you still have the grass skirt?" Insignificant events assume great importance as part of joyous memories of trips to strange and exotic places.

Peace of Mind—Anyone who has traveled has probably encountered at least one exasperating situation, such as losing his luggage en route, being bumped off a flight, or arriving at a hotel to find that there is no record of his reservation. Such traumatic experiences often discourage further travel alone. On escorted tours, the tour manager does the worrying about the luggage arriving with the people. And, since all arrangements have been made in advance for the group, the chance of a person not getting what he ordered is greatly reduced. If something does go wrong, the tour manager is the one who must make it right.

Fear of the Unknown—Being a stranger in a strange place is an uncomfortable feeling for all but the adventurous. Tours provide a knowledgeable person to ease the transition from the known to the unknown. Visits to strange and unusual places may be made with confidence rather than avoided because of the fear of the unknown. It is, therefore, very important that the guide or escort be familiar with all the pertinent facts and able to articulate them to his clients.

What to See and What to Avoid—Choosing between attractions is a major problem for tourists. Brochures describe such places in glowing terms, but some turn out to be disappointing tourist traps. Reputable tour companies, when planning their trips, include only worthwhile sites in their itineraries. A good guide makes sure that the attraction merits the trip and that his clients find it an interesting experience. When certain attractions are omitted from the itinerary for good cause, the guide might explain to his clients why he gave priority to others.

Gaining Knowledge—Another reason people choose escorted tours is to gain knowledge. Many travelers would like to know more about an area they are visiting than is briefly stated in a folder, but they do not have the time, the patience, or perhaps the ability to research this information for themselves. Often they do not have the resources. The tour manager gives them an "in-residence expert" who can provide them with the data they seek. For many people, reading literature about an area is not so interesting as hearing about it from a knowledgeable guide. These tales and legends become especially exciting when told on location; history is better understood and better remembered when associated with a geographical spot.

Cost—Cost is a major factor in attracting people to group tours. The tour operators buy space and contract for services at the trade or wholesale rate. If one calculates the costs of all the items included in a group tour, excluding the tour manager's salary and expenses, one would find the cost per member to be much lower than it would be for an individual paralleling the tour on his own. When one travels in groups, one usually travels wholesale or very close to it. One saves money and trouble. The "package" fare usually is so all-inclusive that it eliminates many extra costs and greatly shrinks the original outlay. Group travel is wholesale travel without worry about details.

Advertising—Travel agencies and transportation companies have pushed escorted tours as the "in" way to travel. Swissair has run advertisements in leading newspapers explaining how tours are put together and sold, as well as insuring that there is a tour for every person.[22] From articles in the travel press, agents learn of the processes and pitfalls involved in making up their own tours.[23]

Canada's Centennial in 1967 and the U.S. Bicentennial in 1976 generated special tours, and the results seem to indicate that people who enjoyed these tours are not likely to return to individual travel. There is excitement in group travel, and the cost is less. Accommodations and services usually are better. Finally, companies well known in other industries are getting into the escorted travel market. One example is the McCall Publishing Company which now offers its readers escorted tours to Europe.[24]

The Tour Manager—An important factor in attracting people to guided tours is certainly the tour manager, the one who provides peace of mind and explains and clarifies strange customs; the host who molds a group of strangers into a community of friends; the history and geography expert who removes the mystery of the unknown. But it is the services rendered over and above the expected that make the tour manager the selling point of group touring. Each travel manager should engage in so-called extracurricular programming to give the tour a plus of favorable memories of pleasant activities. Examples would be the ability to point out "good buys" in each area or to recommend places to eat. Extra excursions might be made to interesting places not mentioned on the itinerary. Or the plus might be just a smile at 6:00 A.M. when there is an early plane to catch. Speaking of their directors, Maupintours says:

> Leadership makes the difference between a mediocre tour and a truly enjoyable, meaningful Maupintour holiday. Maupintour's own Tour Manager knows the country and knows the people and is very experienced in showing American vacationers all that is wonderful and exciting. He will be your pleasant host and good companion and he will make sure you learn to know and love these European countries as well as he does.[25]

Tours and Tour Companies

The modern "escorted tour" had its origin in Leicester, England, in 1841. There, a wood turner by the name of Thomas Cook chartered a train to carry a group of Temperance Society members to a convention in another city. Cook, himself a temperance enthusiast, made all the arrangements for this excursion without taking any profit for his labor. It was his contribution to the cause in which he strongly believed. But as a result of this experience he realized that a living could be made by arranging travel for others. It dawned upon him that people like to have others arrange and organize trips for them, so he made it a business. With this simple step a new profession was conceived and developed that today has become an important industry.

In 1845, Cook left his trade in the carpentry shop and began his new career as a trip organizer. Many of the trips he organized were not escorted. Instead, the traveler was given a voucher to cover his hotel and other expenses, for which arrangements were made in advance. To this day, the voucher method is widely employed.

In 1846, Cook led a tour to neighboring Scotland by train and steamer and prepared an itinerary for each tourist on the trip. Making travel arrangements was now a business for Thomas Cook and Son.

Within twenty years, Cook and Son extended their activities to North America. Thomas Cook himself led a group to "New York, Washington, Richmond, Civil War Battlefields, Mammoth Cave, Cincinnati, Niagara Falls, Toronto and Montreal."[26] It was quite an undertaking. As a result of the many tours Cook organized in all parts of the world, a popular slogan was born: "When you think of travel, think of Cook's."[27]

Success invites competition. Competition and emulation are indeed compliments and endorsement. In the more than six generations since Cook's was founded, the number of tour companies has grown everywhere. In the mid 1970s tour organizing had expanded to such an extent that Eric Friedheim, the editor of *The Travel Agent,* wrote an editorial entitled, "Anyone Can Be a Tour Operator."[28] In it, he pointed out that until recently the tour business "was the province of a few solid outfits nearly all of them with strong fiscal underpinnings and a sound reputation with the trade and public"[29] but that "This year [1977], tour operators are reaching a standing room only condition."[30] Friedheim called for "careful review by industry and government if the best interests of the traveler are to be served."[31]

In addition to the professional tour operators, many transportation companies, such as Greyhound and British Airways, have developed their own tour departments. Special interest groups like the National Education Association organize their own tours on a seasonal and sometimes year-round basis. These tours are limited to members of those organizations and their families. Travel agents and bus brokers also arrange special tours for religious or social groups, usually on a one-time basis. The trade press has been full of articles like "Cashing in on the $200 Billion Singles Market,"[32] or "Group Escorted Motorcoach Tours: A New Avenue for Profit,"[33] all aimed at the local travel agents. The local travel agent thus becomes the first step in organizing an escort's tour. A capable and knowledgeable travel agent with imagination and ideas is in a position to organize interesting, innovative tours that will bring profits to his company and pleasure to his clients.

In the mid-1970s, a drive developed to accommodate people who previously were unable to travel. One such group was the handicapped. The *New York Times* ran a feature article on travel for the handicapped entitled, "The World from a Wheelchair."[34] The article included problems that might be encountered and a list of tours designed for this group. The following year, *Travel Weekly* updated tour information for that same group.[35] Murray Vidockler of All-State Bus Company has organized the Society for the Advancement of Travel for the Handicapped (SATH), which is a travel-industry, nonprofit association to promote and develop more accommodations and tours for the handicapped.[36]

Another group of travelers who have been limited in their touring ability are those persons who follow the kosher dietary laws. This situation is rapidly changing. Geller Howard Travel, Ltd., of New York, for instance, runs tours through North America as well as throughout Europe and has contracted with hotels, far removed from centers of Jewish settlement, to serve meals in accordance with strict Jewish dietary law. According to Geller, domestic and international airlines are also prepared to serve kosher meals on all of their flights if the person or group requiring kosher food requests it when making reservations.[37] Each large center in the world has places or provisions to make it possible for observant Jews to partake of kosher food.

As more tours, specialized and general, are developed, the need for efficient tour managers grows. Many of these new tours require special talents, and the tour manager must prepare accordingly. There will be more and more need for individuals prepared with the special skills to meet the new requirements. The Institute of Transportation, Travel, and Tourism at Niagara University is setting up special courses to familiarize its students with these problems and to prepare them for handling these new, demanding, specialized tours. In time, other schools, too, will adopt these courses.

A tour manager is usually an independent contractor, hired by a certain tour company or agent on a per tour basis. The types of tours offered vary from operator to operator and sometimes even within the same company. The manager must be familiar with the classification of tours in order to prepare to conduct a tour according to its type. The client must receive that which he has contracted for with the company—and the manager should know what these items are. The usual method of classifying tours is to divide them into deluxe, first class, economy, and special (e.g., student) tours.

Deluxe Tours—Deluxe tours stop at only the very best hotels. The membership of such tours is usually limited to between twenty-five and thirty-five people. The clients dine at the finest restaurants with few or no limits on the menu, and the itinerary includes many sight-seeing trips. There are tour operators who specialize in deluxe tours. One of these, speaking about the hotels it patronizes, states: "It has always been our policy to utilize the best possible accommodations on every tour, such as the famed Peninsula Hotel in Hong Kong, and the Imperial in Tokyo. All hotels have a variety of rooms; we utilize only superior rooms. . . ." Their policy on meals is stated as follows:

> Our company knows how delighted people are when offered their choice of meals. That is why we include all meals on an a la carte basis. You may choose whatever you like from an a la carte menu and, in addition, may dine at the many restaurants at our luxury hotels. Take your eating habits with you—eat early or late, individually or in a group, just sign your name, . . .

The company limits its tours to twenty-five people.

Companies offering this type of tour demand the highest

standards of performance from the suppliers and from the tour manager. Such tours are expensive, and the groups are usually composed of wealthy people who have traveled extensively. These are sophisticated clients, who know good service and demand it. However, when something goes wrong over which the manager has no control, these people tend to be the most understanding. Seasoned travelers are cooperative, compassionate, and friendly. They will tolerate genuine miscalculations but will not stand for phony excuses and stupidity.

First Class Tours—First class is one step below deluxe. This type of tour might stay at the Chateau Lake Louise along with a deluxe tour, but the first class tour would occupy mountain-side rooms while the deluxe would occupy those with a lake view. While some first class tours provide meals, most do not. If meals are included, they may be from a special "tour menu" or may be limited to certain items on the regular menu. Or the amount on the check may be limited. The people on this type of tour tend to be middle class and less experienced than those found on a deluxe tour (or they may represent a more frugal group). There are more free nights and open days on this type of tour, and the manager is expected to be able to offer suggestions to his clients to fill this free time.

Economy Tours—Economy tours are just what the name implies. In North America, this designation may mean a room with a bath that must be shared with the adjoining room. Overseas, it may mean a walk to the water closet. In fact, TWA's *Getaway* book states that "budget" (their name for economy) means "hotels without private bath."[38] If any meals are included, they are usually preset. This type of tour tends to move very quickly and appeals to younger people or those on a very tight budget. Economy tours are the least formal of all tours. They represent a lot of fast sight-seeing, much walking, and glimpses of important places rather than presentations in depth.

Special Tours—Tours designed to meet the needs of specific groups are called special tours. Student tours, for example, may stay in college dormitories and have all preset meals. However, there are specially designed tours for special interest groups, and these can fall into any of the other three categories, based upon the accommodations and services needed and offered. Special interest tours are often very sophisticated for they are made up by and for highly intelligent people who are eager to obtain new insights and more knowledge about their specific interests. Catering to these groups requires great ability, and the guide must be a specialist in the fields pursued. With such tours, it is advisable to hire the services of experts in the field.

The tour operator should be able to provide information concerning the type of tour, and the company brochure will offer some clues as to the classification. Large international operators, such as American Express, offer tours in all three classes,[39] and they are so labeled in the brochures.

The tour manager will find that the most difficult tours to classify are those offered by small regional operators or those put together by an independent agent. The literature may classify it as one type of tour, but the itinerary will show it to be something else entirely. In managing this type of a tour, it is well to keep in mind that the suppliers of services may not have had dealings with the company or agency before, and will tend to favor their regular tour customers over a one-time operation. In such cases, it is up to the tour manager to establish a pleasant relationship and good working rapport.

Escorted tours have proliferated in the last decade as more companies have entered the field and more people have been attracted to travel. In addition to the various tour classifications, there are special interest and special need groups deserving of particular attention. The tour manager must be aware of all these things in order to provide the necessary preparation and services. The clients are customers who have paid good money for certain services, and they expect the company's promises to be fulfilled.

QUESTIONS FOR DISCUSSION

1. What justification can be given for calling tour management a profession?

2. What are the major advantages and disadvantages of on-the-job training?
3. Why is common sense so important in this field?
4. What are the ethical responsibilities of a tour manager to his employing company? To the suppliers of services? To his clients?
5. What are the personality traits needed by a tour manager, and what is the importance of each?
6. Why (until recently) has travel always been associated with hardship?
7. The line between travel for business and travel for pleasure has been blurred. Why has this occurred?
8. What role does health play in motivating people to travel?
9. More "minority" people are traveling than ever before. What factors are contributing to this?
10. Why should the tour manager attempt to ascertain why the individual client took his particular tour?
11. What role does companionship play in escorted tours?
12. Why are escorted tours usually less expensive on a per person basis than individual touring?
13. How has advertising helped the growth of the group travel industry?
14. What role does the tour manager play in attracting people to take escorted tours?
15. There has been a great increase in the number of companies offering escorted tours. What are the advantages and disadvantages of this increase?
16. What are "special interest groups," and what are their needs?
17. Discuss the major types of escorted tours and how they differ from each other.
18. Why must the tour manager prepare differently for each type of tour?

NOTES

1. *Travel Weekly*, Apr. 14, 1974, p. 7.
2. Ibid., p. 43.
3. Howard Apter, "Inexperience Can Contribute to Agency Failure," *The Travel Agent*, Feb. 3, 1977, p. 20.
4. Ibid.

5. Grayhound World Tours, Inc., *Escort's Training Manual,* 1975, p. i.
6. William McDougall, *The Group Mind* (New York: G.P. Putnam's Sons, 1920).
7. Gallup Organization, "A Survey of the U.S. Air Traveler," conducted for American Express, Princeton, N.J., 1975, p. 148.
8. "Motor Coach Tours Come of Age," *Travel Weekly,* Sept. 2, 1976, p. 9.
9. "Selling Motorcoach Travel: New Dimensions in Profit," *Travel Trade,* Feature ed., Oct. 4, 1976, p. 6.
10. The International Association of Tour Managers, *Ethics and Principles,* 2nd ed. (London, 1974), p. 5.
11. U.S. Department of Commerce, *1967 Census of Transportation.*
12. Blane Cook, "Travel in the 1970's: The Luxury Market," *Operations Bulletin,* American Hotel and Motel Association, New York, Dec. 1970.
13. *New York Times,* May 9, 1976, p. 1.
14. John A. Thomas, "What Makes People Travel," *ASTA Travel News,* Aug. 1964, pp. 64–65.
15. Donald Lundberg, *The Tourist Business,* 3rd ed. (Boston, CBI Publishing Company, Inc., 1972), pp. 134–148.
16. Ibid., p. 134.
17. Russ Johnson, "Motivation in a Changing Environment," *Operations Bulletin,* American Hotel and Motel Assn., Sept. 1970.
18. Robert B. McCall and Ernest Havermann, *Study Guide to Psychology: An Introduction* (New York: Harcourt Brace Jovanovich, 1972), p. 140.
19. "Pocketa-Pocketa Package Tours," Modern Living section, *Time,* Aug. 9, 1976, p. 74.
20. *New York Times,* Feb. 16, 1975, section 10, p. 23.
21. Donald Lundberg, *The Tourist Business,* 3rd ed. (Boston, CBI Publishing Company, Inc., 1972), p. 145.
22. *Travel Weekly,* Nov. 27, 1975, p. 8D.
23. For examples of these see: *Travel Weekly,* Nov. 13, 1976, p. 27; *Discover America Package Tour Handbook* (Washington, D.C.: Discover America Travel Institute, 1972); *Travel Trade,* Discover America section, Jan. 17, 1977, p. 16.
24. *Travel Weekly,* Dec. 11, 1975, p. 54.
25. Maupintours: *Europe, 1975,* p. 2.
26. "Cook's Started It All," *New York Times,* special supplement, Feb. 6, 1966, p. 1.
27. Ibid.
28. Eric Friedheim, "Anyone Can Be a Tour Operator," *The Travel Agent,* Feb. 7, 1977, p. 82.
29. Ibid.
30. Ibid.
31. Ibid.
32. Thomas F. Hewitt, "Cashing in on the $200 Billion Singles Market," *The Travel Agent,* Jan. 20, 1975, p. 52.
33. John P. Stchnik, "Group Escorted Motorcoach Tours: A New Avenue

for Profit," *Travel Trade,* Discover America section, Jan. 17, 1977, pp. 16–18.

34. "The World from a Wheelchair," *New York Times,* Feb. 23, 1975, section 10, p. 1.

35. *Travel Weekly,* Aug. 30, 1976, p. 8E.

36. For more information, contact Murray Vidockler at All-State Bus Company, 26 Court St., Brooklyn, N.Y.

37. Conversation with the author, Mar. 17, 1977.

38. Trans World Airlines, *TWA Getaway, 1975,* p. 31.

39. For a good example, see American Express, *1977 Europe,* Grand-Deluxe; Priceless-First Class; Carefree-Tourist.

PART 3

Preparations: What the Client Never Sees

The job of tour conducting is much like the job of teaching; the escort can make it easy or hard, depending upon his approach . . .
Greyhound World Tours, *Escort's Training Manual,* 1975

4. PRETOUR PREPARATION

A teacher first outlines and researches his objectives for a course and then decides on the manner of successfully achieving them. He prepares his daily lesson plans, devises methods of evaluating his progress, marks his tests, and so on. For the tour manager as well as the teacher, efficiency in advance preparation is essential. Like the teacher, the tour manager must set objectives in advance and then make sure they are effectively realized. This involves confirming reservations, writing out reports, evaluating services, and much more. Not everyone involved in the travel industry fully understands and appreciates the extent of this out-of-sight work.[1]

A tour manager's work begins long before he meets the people he will be escorting. Advance preparation by the individual manager is the keystone upon which a successful tour is run. We cannot overemphasize this point. The better the preparation, the more smoothly the tour will run. No tour manager can establish himself as a leader if he cannot answer the many questions clients usually ask about an area included in the tour. All the necessary facts are available to be researched, studied, and classified for easy and constant reference. To be effective, a manager must be knowledgeable, organized, and prepared for any eventuality.

In addition to researching a region's history and statistics, the manager should know what consumer goods the area is noted for and where these may be obtained at fair prices. He should be aware of the local restaurants (when meals are not included in the tour), nightclubs, and other forms of entertainment. This sort of information is what establishes the manager's expertise. The clients will expect their manager to supply these facts with authority and speed.

Sources of Information

When you sign a contract to manage a tour, you should, at the same time, find out what type of tour it is (deluxe, first class, economy, special) and, if possible, obtain an idea of the people

who will be on it, their ages, ethnic affiliations, and other partic-
ulars. (This is not always possible, but you may find, for example,
that a travel agent has booked a Golden Age club as part of a
larger tour.) Make sure you have a copy of the exact working
itinerary (this gives departure times, mileages, highway numbers,
and so on) and a copy of the itinerary that was given to the
clients. These are two different itineraries, each detailing different
items and information. Also obtain a copy of the company's
manual for escorts; this will be your bible. Read these materials
carefully, and do not hesitate to ask any questions that may come
to mind. Make certain that you understand everything. Sometimes you will find a discrepancy between the client itinerary and
the working brochure. The client's itinerary is printed well in
advance of the company's final arrangements, and there is often
no time or opportunity to update it. Point out any discrepancy to
the company representative, and find out whether the clients were
notified of the change. Most of the larger tour operators will
notify the clients of such changes, but if they have not, you will
have to explain to the group and advance a good and honest
reason for the change. All arrangements and schedules are subject
to change without notice, but that does not mean that those
affected need not be apprised of these changes.

With the working itinerary in your possession, you are now
ready to begin your research. The best and most reliable source of
up-to-date information on any Canadian province or U.S. state is
the provincial or state tourist office, usually located in the capital
city.[2] These offices are very prompt in mailing maps and other
material on request. The national airlines and tourist bureaus
connected with the embassies or consulates are invaluable sources
of information about other countries. The more details you can
supply them regarding the itinerary and the makeup of your
group, the more helpful will be the information they will supply
to you. This is particularly true if you have a special interest
group, such as architects or lawyers. The airlines have offices in
most major cities; so do the consulates.

Commercially produced guidebooks or brochures are good
sources of information. Some of the oil companies have published
excellent regional guides to North America, one of the better

known ones being the *Mobil Travel Guide.*[3] This guide includes listings and ratings of hotels in every community in the region and gives the community's population, points of interest, and history, along with a calendar of special events. For their members, automobile or motor clubs are another invaluable source of information. For travel outside North America, too, there are some excellent guides. The companies you will be working for probably have them in their libraries. The more you read about the places you will be visiting, the more informed you will be.

For historical background on the American states, you should look for the federal *Writer's Guide* for each state, published during the Depression by the U.S. government. Access to a good library is helpful in obtaining background information of all kinds. Use the library in your own city always! Do not forget the *National Geographic* magazines. They are superb.

No matter how well you prepare for the trip, you cannot be a walking expert on all the places you visit. People will ask you many questions you will not be able to answer. When that happens, as it often will, try to find the information as soon as possible. Local guides usually are the best sources of on-the-spot information. Make their acquaintance. They are all friendly and very cooperative.

What kind of information should you prepare? The following list is cited as a guide to start you on your way.

I.   Know the answers to the following questions about the hotels at which you will be staying:
   A.   Is the hotel in the heart of town, or is it in the outskirts?
   B.   Are there any points of interest near the hotel?
   C.   Will your tour be in town when the stores are open at night, and if so, where are the stores in relation to the hotel?
   D.   How nearby is public transportation to town or to stores?
   E.   If it is a Saturday-night–Sunday-morning stopover, where are the churches, and what are the schedules of the services? (You can get this information at the time you call the hotels to reconfirm your reservations.)

F. Does the hotel have a pool or other special activities for guests?

II. Know the following facts about the cities in which you make overnight stops:

A. General description of the city, for example, size, major industries, points of interest; locations of shopping centers, movie houses, places for dancing and other entertainment, and so on; a list of good restaurants in various price ranges, including the hotel's restaurant, if hotel meals are not included in the tour package.

B. If free time is available, the location and hours of museums, local sight-seeing trips, special stores, and other places of interest.

III. Know the population and major historic facts about the cities you will be passing through on your way to a definite destination.

IV. Find out the major crops of any agricultural regions you will pass through.

In brief, prepare information by using common sense. People are interested in almost everything. Some people have special interests in specific matters. There will be many in your group who will want to hear what you have to say about the countryside and your destinations. Try to determine what the average person coming into a region for the first time would want to know. If you have a special tour (e.g., teachers), try to find out information that would be of interest to that group. Tailor your talks to the group you are leading. Basically, all these narratives are the same with added information for special groups. If you know whom you will have on your trip, try to be prepared for them.

The Tour Manager's Information Log

The information log is a systematic way of recording the information you will need day by day while on tour. Obtain a small, pocket-size, loose-leaf notebook and a supply of pages. Designate a page for each day of the tour, and on the top of each page put the number of the day of the tour as well as the date and day of the week. This will assure the chronological order of the information.

Using the tour itinerary, record the starting point, leave space, record the lunch stop, and then, near the bottom, record the name and location of the hotel where you will be staying that night. In between, record any stops scheduled to be made that day. Using the remaining space, record the information you have researched. It is always wise to record on the bottom of the back of the page the sources of your information. You must have authority for what you are telling your people. Often, you will have clients who want to read more about a certain place they have visited, and you can then tell them where to find the information. You will discover, too, that some clients have done their own research and know more about the subject than you do. Be prepared to use these people as sources of much helpful information.

You must keep your log with you at all times and update it constantly as the tour progresses. You will find the time you spend keeping this up to date a good investment. When the tour is over, file the pages for future reference, and you will have a basic store of information which you can review and update whenever you conduct another tour in the same region. Since most tours are basically the same as far as technical problems are concerned, this system of review will reduce the amount of time that you must spend in repeated research and will insure your having accurate information at your fingertips at all times. Good planning is the mark of a good guide.

Wardrobe and Packing

Another important part of your pretour preparation is the selection of your wardrobe. Many tours limit the number of suitcases you may carry, and airlines limit the weight of your luggage. To look fresh and well-groomed at all times, select clothing that is easy to care for, keeps its shape, and is as lightweight as possible.

DAY 3   WEDNESDAY   MAY 27

9 A.M. – DEPART N.Y.C. (STATLER HOTEL)
          G.W. BRIDGE
          THRUWAY FACTS
          DUTCH IN HUDSON VALLEY

10:30 – REST STOP N.Y. THRUWAY
          TALK ABOUT ALBANY

NOON – ALBANY – TOUR OF CAPITAL

1:00 – LUNCH (JACK'S REST)
          ERIE CANAL
          FORT STANWIX

3:30 - REST STOP N.Y. THRUWAY
          PAS PRTS FOR CANADA
          COMFORTABLE SHOES

5:30 - ARRIVE ROCHESTER (HOLIDAY INN)

Figure 1. Page of Tour Manager's Information Log

The type of tour will partly determine the style of clothing you select. For example, you will need more formal attire on a deluxe tour than on a first class tour, where a casual wardrobe would be in order. The climate of the areas you will be visiting will also be an important factor in determining the type of clothing you will choose for any particular tour. As Dr. Kevin Cahill points out: "Native clothing is another reflection of the effort of mankind to minimize the adverse effects of climatic extremes. The flowing cotton garb of the Bedouin in the desert permits maximum protection from the sun's rays and provides the most efficient ventilation possible."[4]

Today, with the advent of the so-called miracle fabrics, living out of a suitcase is not the problem it once was. However, one point of caution is in order here: many of the man-made fibers hold in body heat, while cotton does not, and cotton absorbs perspiration. Therefore, cotton is still the coolest fabric to wear in hot climates. Cotton requires more care than the miracle fabrics, but this is not a problem in areas where wearing cotton is a necessity because "hand labor is one of the most available commodities in most of the developing parts of the world and laundry services are rapid and inexpensive."[5]

For traveling in temperate climates, the so-called wash-and-wear fabrics are a blessing. Some of the more popular ones are:

1. *Acetate:* mainly used in women's dresses, blouses, and lingerie. Generally, it should be dry-cleaned. If washed, it must be pressed at the lowest possible heat. It is adversely affected by nail polish remover and some perfumes.
2. *Acrylic:* popular in socks, sport clothes, and sweaters. It should be washed with a fabric softener.
3. *Olefin:* used in some sportswear. It must be washed gently, and it cannot be dried in a commercial (Laundromat) gas-fired dryer.
4. *Polyester:* the "permanent press" fabric. It is machine washable and dryable and needs little, if any, ironing; shrinks with constant washing.[6]

Hotel laundries use extremely hot water and strong cleaning

agents with the result that wash-and-wear items may lose their permanent press after a few washings. Polyester pops in very hot water, so it is inadvisable to have garments made of these man-made fibers laundered by the hotel. You will find it to your advantage to wear any item of clothing made of synthetic fiber for only a short period of time and then wash it out yourself.

Cotton, in addition to being the best fabric to wear in hot climates, is the best fabric to wear next to the skin in cold climates. It allows the body to "breathe," and it absorbs moisture much better than synthetics. For trips to cold climates, dressing in layers is suggested, for example, cotton underwear, cotton shirt or blouse, wool or synthetic sweater, and so on. Dressed in this manner, one can shed or add layers as conditions change from one stop to the next.

Choosing colors that coordinate easily will keep the amount of clothing you need to a minimum because you will be able to mix and match garments rather than having to provide for completely separate outfits for each day.

A good raincoat is essential for any tour. You will be at the door of the bus to assist people in and out. You also must supervise the loading and unloading of the baggage and count pieces of luggage each time. Both of these jobs are often done in pouring rain. A good raincoat thus becomes a necessary investment.

It seems almost too obvious to include the importance of good, comfortable shoes to a tour manager. A major part of your day will be spent on your feet walking through exhibits, gardens, historic sites, and other places of interest. You will not be able to do your job effectively if your feet hurt. Your shoes and also your socks are, therefore, among the most important parts of your wardrobe, and you will need at least one change of shoes to keep at peak efficiency. Shoes should always be cleaned and/or shined at the beginning of the day.

After you have chosen your wardrobe, the next logical step is packing. Your luggage is best kept to one medium-sized suitcase plus an overnight or flight bag. Experienced tour managers can pack a surprising amount of clothing in these two pieces. Utilize every inch by packing socks inside shoes, rolling underwear to "stuff" around other garments, and so on. Use your flight bag for your toilet articles (which should all be packaged in plastic containers) and for your nightclothes.[7]

You will probably find it more efficient if, each evening on tour, you lay out your outfit for the next day and then pack your suitcase. Then, in the morning, you have only to pack your flight bag. It is not uncommon for hotels to give all of the tour members a wake-up call and forget to call the manager. If all you have to pack are your toilet articles and your nightclothes, you can be ready in a few minutes. (Of course, you should not allow this to happen; make sure you will be awakened.)

Proper planning is the key to success in any endeavor—and especially when taking a group of people with you on a tour. Plan for each tour by familiarizing yourself with the type of tour you will be conducting, the exact itinerary, and the material contained in the company's escort manual. Study the places you will be visiting, and be prepared to answer general questions about them. Use the tour manager's information log to organize this information. Select your wardrobe carefully so that you will be comfortable and look your best at all times.

Your appearance, your patience, your authority, your knowledge, and your behavior all contribute to the success or failure of a tour. Inattention to these details will convert a tour into an irritating experience and result in dissatisfied clients.

5. RECONFIRMATION CALLS

True professionalism becomes evident in the area of reconfirmation calls. Some groups of leaders erroneously believe that a service will be insured just because they are holding the vouchers in their possession. These "escorts" are deceiving themselves and inviting trouble. Reconfirming reservations is a must. Have you ever seen an escort who has just arrived at a hotel with his group and finds that there is no record of the tour and the house is booked solid? Fortunately, such situations do not happen when a knowledgeable professional person is in charge.

Reconfirmation calls are so named because the manager is reconfirming, or following up, a company's order (voucher) for a service. He is, in effect, validating the original order by making such a call. These calls are company policy for most tour operators. "Each service must be reconfirmed, wherever possible, by telephone no later than 48 hours before arrival or prior to use of services (transportation, hotels, meals, special occasions and sightseeing)."[8]

If you should be employed by a company, group, or agent who does not list these calls in your expense account, request that an amount be added to cover such calls. It is a legitimate expense, extremely necessary, and you will do yourself and your company a great favor by making advance provisions to have funds for it.

Hotels should always be called at least forty-eight hours before your arrival. When you place your call, have the voucher in front of you, ask for the person who manages tour bookings (the name is usually on the voucher), and speak to him clearly and with authority.

1. Give him your name.
2. Give him the company and tour name and/or number of the tour.
3. Detail the actual needs of the tour—the number of singles, twins, and so on.
4. Advise him if there is a change from the original and, if so, give the change of names.

5. Advise him of your estimated time of arrival and any special needs. The more you tell him, the easier it will be for you.

Calls to reconfirm meals should be made at least twenty-four hours prior to arrival. Give the restaurants the same information as above and alert them should you have clients who have special dietary needs and problems. You must ascertain these things at the first meeting with your group. Sight-seeing and transportation calls should be handled in the same manner as restaurant calls. A telephone call in time will save you time, money, energy, and aggravation.

On the voucher, record the date and time of these calls *and* the name of the person with whom you spoke. Pinpointing responsibility is a major factor in obtaining good services.

When a service manager has no record of the tour's reservation, ask the person to whom you are speaking to recheck his records, and give him a number and a location where you can be reached. Give him the date on your voucher and any other information he may seek. Make it easy for him to save face and help you. Be sure to ask him if the tour can be accommodated. If he calls you back and says that it cannot, notify your company at once. Give the company the name of the person to whom you have spoken, and if you are familiar with the area suggest possible alternatives. Leave a number where you can be reached. It is the tour company's responsibility to work out the dilemma, find alternate solutions, and contact you. But you are the one to whom the complaints, criticism, or compliments will be directed by the travelers.

Under no circumstances should you indicate to the clients that there is the possibility of a problem. They should not be involved. Any situation that might be troublesome can usually be straightened out by the time the service is to be rendered if you make your reconfirmation calls on time. As far as the clients are concerned, the trip was smooth and sans problems.

If the service managers have no record of your tour but can accommodate you, give them all of the information and follow up with a reconfirmation call the following day. Also notify your office of the problem and the action you have taken. Keep your office apprised of all your problems and solutions.

Ticketing

The tour manager generally receives custody of the airline, ship, rail, or bus tickets for the group either at the company office or at the departure site. When the tickets are received, the spacing must be matched with the number of tour participants. If the tickets are for several moves, each move must be verified by checking the coupons on each ticket to insure that there is a voucher or coupon for each move. Lastly, it is imperative to check the dates on the tickets. Many tours have arrived at terminals only to discover that the tickets were issued for the following day and there is no space available for that day. Calling in advance for reconfirmation will help to avoid this situation.

If you are in doubt about how to read a ticket, ask someone in the company office to explain the symbols, abbreviations, and so on, to you. If you receive the tickets at the departure site and the office help is not available, you should ask someone from the airline or rail system to help you.

Be conscious of people who are joining the tour en route. Determine who has tickets and where you will receive custody of them.

Singles and Twins

People traveling alone on tours somehow feel that they are second-class citizens. Make every effort to dispel that notion from the start. Avoid having singles sit by themselves. Do not allow them to feel that they are alone. On the first day, begin by joining them for a meal. Learn their names, and introduce them to other people on the tour. When giving out room keys, always start with the singles' keys first.

Some resort hotels have set a limit on the number of single rooms a tour can book. Fortunately, most tour companies stress this fact and call it to your attention in their brochures. Should you have a large number of singles on one particular tour and suspect that it may exceed the limit, mention this fact in a general way to the whole group early in the tour. You might find that two from your group will volunteer to share a room if there are insufficient singles. Experienced escorts note the singles who have become friendly during the tour and put them together when rooms must be shared. Should you encounter this situation at more than one hotel, try to pair different people each time.

When you place the reconfirmation request, determine then and there if single rooms are available and note any differential in rates.

Many companies will accept singles on a share basis. This means that the client is willing to share accommodations with another single client who has joined the tour. Sometimes this arrangement is satisfactory. Occasionally, a personality conflict will develop en route, and one or both will insist on single accommodations for the balance of the tour. The policy of most companies requires any person requesting single accommodations to pay, in cash, directly to the hotels the additional charge for these accommodations.

When two singles, on the other hand, express a desire to share a room for the balance of the tour, you should try to help them. Make the request when you place your reconfirmation calls to the hotels. Advise the company of the clients' decision, also. Any refunds due the single clients who are now sharing the room should be handled by the tour company office, not by you. Tell your clients that you have notified the company of their decision and that it is up to them to contact the company directly upon returning home.

6. BORDER CROSSINGS

For many people, crossing an international frontier is a traumatic experience. One tourist said, "It is like being called down to the income tax office for an audit. You know that your records are in order, but you are still scared."[9] People take guided tours because they want a "peace of mind trip, clear of worries, troubles and the need to make decisions." Your job is to help them achieve this and reduce any anxiety. Assure the group that you will precede them, and advise the authorities that they are part of a tour and that you will give the immigration officials all the required information about the group. Make your clients feel at ease.

A tour manager quickly becomes an expert on passports and visas. Fortunately, most tour companies advise their clients of the documentation they will need on any particular trip. Occasionally, a slip-up will occur. One major company operated a guided tour of the northeastern United States that included a visit to the Canadian side of Niagara Falls but failed to include in the brochure the need for citizenship identification. Crossing from the U.S.A. into Canada is going into a foreign country, and citizenship proof is necessary. When you contract to manage a tour, check the brochure carefully and, should you find an omission or error, call it to the attention of the management. Attempt to have the correct information sent to those already booked and revised information given to all new bookings.

North America

The basic requirement for citizens of Canada or the United States visiting one another's country is proof of citizenship. While drivers' licenses, social insurance or social security cards are not legally sufficient for the purpose, these documents are sometimes accepted by immigration authorities for tour members. They may, however, cause a slight delay. Proper legal identification would be a birth certificate, naturalization papers, a baptismal record, a passport (even if expired), or a voter's registration card.

If a citizen of a country other than the United States or Canada is on your tour, check his passport to see that it will be valid for the duration of the tour. Note the expiration date, and find out whether he has a visa. For visitors coming to the United States, there are two types of visas: single entry and multiple entry. If a tour organization is going from Canada into the States, a single entry visa is sufficient. However, if the tour originates in the United States and is going into Canada and the client has a single entry visa, he will have already used that visa period when he entered the U.S. originally. Another permit will be needed for reentry from Canada. Stop at the U.S. immigration station *before* crossing into Canada to check the situation with the immigration officer on duty. He may endorse the visa, allowing the person to reenter the U.S., but he may refuse such an endorsement. If the tour will be visiting a Canadian city with an American consulate, the client may be able to get the visa changed to multiple entry, but this is not an automatic process. You must clear these things prior to crossing the border. The decision to leave the U.S. and attempt this change *must be made by the client.*

People of Latin American origin have a particular problem. The U.S. Immigration Service, conscious of illegal immigrants, tends to check their documentation more thoroughly than that of people from other areas. If you have any doubts about the sufficiency of the credentials of anyone on your tour, check before you cross the border. Be safe and inquire; avoid problems and complications.

Immigration authorities do expedite tours crossing their borders, especially if the tour is returning to its country of origin. If all members are completing the tour, the officials are most considerate about the documentation required and may even accept a tour list showing home addresses and the tour manager's statement. But you should not count on this—check and double check.

If you will be returning to Canada or the United States through the same checkpoint on a regular basis, it is advisable to ask the immigration officer if there is anything you can do to help him expedite crossings. Some points, like the U.S. Customs Office at Big Chief Mountain in Glacier International Park, have special forms for tours. You may ask the passengers to fill out the form

Car No. _____

Lic. No. _____

Manifest No. _____

Sheet No. _____

Arrived at Port of, _____

on _____

Inward Manifest of Automobiles

Tour No. _____

Time _____ A.M. / P.M.

REPORT MANIFEST AND LIST OF PASSENGERS AND BAGGAGE TAKEN ON BOARD AUTO NO. _____ AT WATERTON LAKES, ALBERTA, CANADA, WHEREOF _____ is the person in charge. Destination, Glacier Park, Montana, U. S. A. For entry at U. S. Customs station of Chief Mountain, Montana. Auto Stage owned and operated by Glacier Park Transport Company, East Glacier Park, Montana.

NAME OF PASSENGER	CITY	STATE OR COUNTRY	DESTINATION (IF NOT CITIZEN OF U. S.)	TIME REMAINING IN U. S. (IF NOT CITIZEN OF U. S.)	DECLARATION OF GOODS OR MERCHANDISE OBTAINED ABROAD	
					PURCHASES	TOTAL VALUE
1						
2						
3						
4						
5						
6						
7						
8						
9						
10						
11						
12						
13						
14						
15						
16						
17						
18						

Declaration of Person in Charge of Vehicle:

I hereby declare that there are _____ pieces of baggage or merchandise which are not accompanied by the owner, and I do solemnly swear that the report and manifest subscribed in my name, and now delivered by me to the Collector of Customs of the port named above, contains, to the best of my knowledge and belief, a just and true account of all the goods, wares, and merchandise, including packages of every kind and nature whatsoever, which constitute the contents of lading of the vehicle named above; that the said manifest contains a just and true account of all the lading of said vehicle when the same first arrived within the limits of the United States, and that I have been, since the arrival of said vessel or vehicle within the United States, master or person in charge of said vehicle, and that no packages whatsoever, nor any goods, wares, or merchandise have been taken out, unladen, or in any way removed from said vehicle since its arrival within the United States.

And I further swear that if I shall hereafter discover or know of any other or greater quantity of goods, wares, or merchandise of any kind and nature whatsoever than is contained in the report and manifest subscribed to and now delivered by me, I will immediately and without delay make due report thereof to the Collector of the district named above.

Subscribed and sworn to before me this _____ day of _____, 19____.

_____
Deputy Collector of Customs.

GLACIER PARK TRANSPORT COMPANY

By _____

FORM 11—TRIBUNE 6648

Figure 2. Inward Manifest of Automobiles

before arrival at the checkpoint. Cooperation with these officials will not only smooth your crossings but ensure consideration should problems develop, as they easily might.

Latin America and Overseas

Tourists traveling to Latin America and overseas are required to carry tourist cards and/or passports and/or visas. As part of your own preparations, you must get your own documentation in order. This experience will acquaint you with what is required of the clients. One of the best sources for up-to-date immigration requirements is *The Pan American Immigration Guide*,[10] which is available for perusal at any Pan American Airways ticket office. Include this information in your tour manager's information log. Check your clients' documentation at the time of their initial registration prior to the departure of the tour. One tour company gives the following instructions to its managers:

Necessary Documents: You must verify the validity of all travel documents on international tours. However, you should give them back to your tour members following your inspection. These documents are very important and you must not be responsible for their loss (such as theft, etc. . . . this has happened before!!!)

1. U.S. passports are valid for five years. Make sure tour members' passports are valid for the duration of the tour.
2. Record all tour members' passport numbers on a rooming list.
3. Make sure clients have procured all necessary visas; if you have non-U.S. citizens on your tour, verify their visa requirements with the airlines or the Four Winds representatives.
4. On Latin American tours, make sure tour members have all the necessary tourist cards.
5. Verify all International Health Certificates. They must bear the stamp of the Department of Health.
6. If a tour member's documents are not in order, assist him/her in obtaining the proper papers at next destination. The tour member is responsible for costs involved, such as taxi fare, visa fees, etc.[11]

Immigration Procedures

When you debark or arrive at an immigration station, assemble the tour as a group. You should precede them from the plane or ship, with your papers ready for the immigration official. You will need a list of tour members with their home cities and individual citizenships. The list should indicate the amount of time the tour will be staying in that country and the departure point and date. Give the agent the name of the tour and your name, and inform him that *you* are the tour manager. If any member of the tour is terminating (leaving the tour) while in that country, inform the inspector of that fact and give him the client's name. Leave nothing out. Avoid future entanglements with the immigration laws.

Customs Procedures Abroad

It is important that the tour manager keep abreast of the customs regulations of the countries the tour will be visiting. These do change from time to time, but accurate up-to-date information is readily available from several sources. Among them are the airline representative, *The Pan American Immigration Guide,* and the duty-free shop at the airport (these shops deal with customs problems all day long). Apprise your clients of the customs regulations, the limits of their purchases, the currency regulations, and so on, the day before you enter the country, if possible. Do not leave these details to the last minute.

Customs Procedures Returning Home

Know Before You Go[12] is not only good advice to a tour manager but also the title of a booklet issued by the United States Customs Service to residents traveling outside the United States. Get it. Use it. Study it. Canada Customs issues a booklet, *I Declare (Je déclare)*, as a service to Canadian residents.[13] You must know the regulations that will apply to your tour upon returning home, so obtain a copy of the appropriate booklet and keep it with you. All regulations change from time to time, so it is best to pick up a new copy occasionally. Go over the regulations with the entire group early in the tour.

At the customs office, follow the same procedure as stated above for clearing immigration. You should be checked first, and the tour members should be immediately behind you. Give the official all the information about the tour, its length of stay outside the country, nations visited, and so on. Identify the group's luggage, and in any other way possible help expedite the members' passage. Customs forms are usually given out on the plane or ship before arrival. You will be requested to assist the tour members in filling out these forms. Become familiar with these documents, and you will have no trouble.

Tour Manager's Clearance

A special note must be included regarding your own customs procedures. Unlike the clients who cross frontiers only on occasional vacations, many tour managers cross them on a regular basis as a necessary part of earning their livelihood.

Managers who are Canadian residents are allowed the benefits of the ordinary Canadian tourist.[14] In addition, they are covered by section 703-13-1 of the Canada Customs regulations. Tour managers who are residents of the U.S. have the same basic allowances as those allotted to all U.S. residents.[15] A manager who has used his exemption on a previous trip is permitted a limited tobacco and alcohol allowance provided he is going out of the U.S. on another tour. This is called the "crew exemption."[16]

It is incumbent upon you to keep a record of your border crossings and the dates that you claimed your exemptions. If you are in doubt about your eligibility to claim an exemption for purchases on any particular trip, ask a customs official. He will review the regulations for you. You, least of all, can afford to become involved in infractions of customs laws.

Avoid carrying packages for other people who want you to take a "gift" into another country for them. You may not know what the gift is and may find you are carrying contraband. You cannot

DEPARTMENT OF THE TREASURY
UNITED STATES CUSTOMS SERVICE

CUSTOMS DECLARATION

FORM APPROVED
O.M.B. NO. 48-R0386

PRESENT TO THE IMMIGRATION AND CUSTOMS INSPECTORS
EACH ARRIVING TRAVELER OR HEAD OF A FAMILY MUST WRITE IN THE FOL-
LOWING INFORMATION. **PLEASE PRINT**

1. FAMILY NAME	GIVEN NAME	MIDDLE INITIAL

2. DATE OF BIRTH (Mo./Day/Yr.)	3. VESSEL, OR AIRLINE & FLT. NO.

4. CITIZEN OF (Country)	5. RESIDENT OF (Country)

6. PERMANENT ADDRESS

7. ADDRESS WHILE IN THE UNITED STATES

8. NAME AND RELATIONSHIP OF ACCOMPANYING FAMILY MEMBERS

9. ARE YOU OR ANYONE IN YOUR PARTY CARRYING ANY FRUITS, PLANTS, MEATS, OTHER PLANT OR ANIMAL PRODUCTS, BIRDS OR OTHER LIVE ORGANISMS OF ANY KIND?	☐ YES	☐ NO
10. ARE YOU OR ANYONE IN YOUR PARTY CARRYING OVER $5000.00 IN COIN, CURRENCY, OR MONETARY INSTRUMENTS?	☐ YES	☐ NO

11. *I CERTIFY THAT I HAVE DECLARED ALL ITEMS ACQUIRED ABROAD AS RE-
QUIRED HEREIN, AND THAT ALL ORAL AND WRITTEN STATEMENTS WHICH
I HAVE MADE ARE TRUE, CORRECT AND COMPLETE.*

SIGNATURE:

NON-CITIZENS ONLY	12. U.S. VISA ISSUED AT (Place)	13. VISA DATE (Mo./Day/Yr.)

In addition, the laws of the United States require that you declare **ALL articles acquired abroad** *(whether worn or used, whether dutiable or not, and whether obtained by purchase, as a gift, or otherwise)* which are in your or your family's possession
at the time of arrival. Furthermore, **Repairs made abroad must also be declared.**

Nonresidents may make an oral declaration. **Returning Residents** may make an
oral declaration if the total price of articles declared *(price actually paid or, if not
purchased, fair retail price in country where obtained)* is not more than the sum of
$100 per person. Otherwise **You Must List In Writing On The Reverse Of This Form
All Articles And Repairs Acquired Abroad Which You Are Now Bringing Through
Customs.** *(See additional instructions on reverse.)*

All your baggage *(including handbags and hand-carried parcels)* may be examined.
False Statements Made To A Customs Officer Are Punishable By Law. Consult
"U.S. Customs Hints" and your inspector for full information.

OFFICIAL USE ONLY

STAMP NOS.

NO. PCS. BAGGAGE EXMD.	TIME COMPLETED
INSPECTOR	
DATE	BADGE NO.

CUSTOMS FORM 6059-B (8-23-74)

Figure 3. United States Customs Declaration Form:
both sides

DESCRIPTION OF ARTICLES	PRICE	CUSTOMS USE ONLY
TOTAL PRICE		

Attach Continuation Sheets If Necessary

State price ACTUALLY PAID. If not purchased, state fair price in country where obtained. You may combine articles costing less than $5 each and list as MISCELLANEOUS up to a total of $50. List separately all other items regardless of cost.

THIS SPACE RESERVED FOR VALIDATION

Revenue Canada
Customs and Excise

Revenu Canada
Douanes et Accise

REF. NO
Nº DE RÉFÉRENCE
0600790

| MR | MRS | MISS |
| M. | MME | MLLE |

FAMILY OR LAST NAME / FIRST NAMES

NOM DE FAMILLE / PRÉNOM(S)

ADDRESS
ADRESSE

NUMBER, STREET, APT. NO., P.O. BOX NO., OR R.R. NO.

NUMÉRO, RUE, Nº D'APP., CASE POSTALE OU ROUTE RURALE

CITY, TOWN OR VILLAGE, COUNTY OR RURAL MUNICIPALITY

VILLE OU VILLAGE, COMTÉ OU MUNICIPALITÉ RURALE

PROVINCE

PROVINCE

DATE OF DEPARTURE FROM CANADA
DATE DE DÉPART DU CANADA

MONTH/MOIS   DAY/JOUR   19

ARE YOU IMPORTING ANY MEATS, PLANTS OR PLANT MATERIAL?

IMPORTEZ VOUS DES VIANDES, DES PLANTES OU DES MATIÈRES VÉGÉTALES?

YES ☐   NO ☐
OUI   NON

COUNTRY WHERE THE MAJORITY OF THE GOODS WERE ACQUIRED

PAYS OU LA MAJEURE PARTIE DES MARCHANDISES A ÉTÉ ACQUISE

U.S.A ☐   OTHER ☐
E.U   AUTRE

THE VALUE OF ALL ARTICLES PURCHASED OR RECEIVED ABROAD MUST BE DECLARED

IL FAUT DÉCLARER LA VALEUR DE TOUS LES ARTICLES ACHETÉS OU REÇUS À L'ÉTRANGER

VALUE OF GOODS CARRIED IN HAND AND CHECKED BAGGAGE $

VALEUR DES MARCHANDISES DANS LES BAGAGES À MAIN OU ENREGISTRÉS

VALUE OF GOODS SHIPPED TO ARRIVE AT A LATER DATE $

VALEUR DES MARCHANDISES EXPÉDIÉES ET DEVANT ARRIVER PLUS TARD

TOTAL VALUE $
VALEUR GLOBALE

☐ 70310-1   ☐ 70311-1

....
Signature of Claimant/Signature du demandeur

FOR CUSTOMS USE ONLY / À L'USAGE DES DOUANES

VALUE OF GOODS
VALEUR DES
MARCHANDISES

MANIFEST NO
Nº DU
MANIFESTE

SIGNATURE OF CLAIMANT
SIGNATURE DU DEMANDEUR

PORT DATE STAMP
TIMBRE DATEUR DU BUREAU

E 24 (8/74)

Figure 4. Revenue Canada, Customs and Excise

afford a favor that may jeopardize your job. Carry only your own belongings, and if you are bringing a gift to anyone, declare it. Your job is to speed people through, not delay them with your own customs problems.

Currency Exchange

Currency exchange is an operation with .which many tourists feel uncomfortable. It is confusing and often requires a bit of arithmetic. The rate of exchange is not constant, and indeed, the rates often vary on the same day from place to place. In addition, there is a language barrier.

You, the tour manager, should become familiar with the currency of the countries you will be visiting and the approximate exchange rates. If you have purchased small amounts of currency in advance, you can use them to familiarize your group with the new money. *Travel Weekly* and those major daily newspapers with a complete financial section list exchange rates.

Most tourists carry travelers' checks and internationally recognized credit cards rather than cash. Tour members will, however, need small amounts of local currency for tips, postcards, stamps, and so on. Before entering a new country, show the group a representative sample of the money used there. If a different numerical system is used (for example, in the Arabian countries), show the group how the basic numbers (1, 2, 5, 10, etc.) are written. The tourists will enjoy the learning experience and will benefit from it.

It is best for your clients to convert small sums of their currency at the hotel cashier's desk, even though the hotel charges for this service and adds a percentage. Your clients may prefer the slight rate difference to a walk to a bank where they may run into a language problem. Larger sums for major purchases, however, should be converted at a bank, as the savings will be considerable. Airports, too, have banks or money exchange offices for the convenience of travelers. Advise your clients to spend whatever coins they have before leaving; it is difficult to exchange the coinage once you leave that country.

NUMERALS

	1	2	3	4	5	6	7	8	9	0	10	100	1000
ARABIC-TURKISH	١	٢	٣	٤	٥	٦	٧	٨	٩	·	١·	١··	١···
MALAY PERSIAN	١	٢	٣	٤	٥	٦	٧	٨	٩	·			
CHINESE, JAPANESE, KOREAN, ANNAMESE (Ordinary)	一	二	三	四	五	六	七	八	九		十	百	千
CHINESE, JAPANESE, KOREAN, ANNAMESE (Official)	壹	貳	叄	肆	伍	陸	柒	捌	玖		拾	(半=½)	仟
INDIAN	९	२	३	४	५	६	७	८	९	0	ၜ	ၜ	
SIAMESE	๑	๒	๓	๔	๕	๖	๗	๘	๙	0	๑๐	๑๐๐	
BURMESE	၁	၂	၃	၄	၅	၆	၇	၈	၉	0			

Figure 5. Chart of Foreign Numerals
Source: R.S. Yeoman, A Catalogue of Modern World Coins, *6th edition, (Racine, Wisc.: Whitman Publishing Co., 1964), p. 5.*

There is an active black market in currency exchange in many countries. Warn the travelers against using it. It is also illegal to bring local currency into some countries (e.g., rubles may not be brought into the U.S.S.R.). Never endanger the safety of clients or put yourself in jeopardy by encouraging or engaging in these profitable but illegal activities. The consequence can be a very bitter experience. An entire group of people may suffer because of the misconduct of one thoughtless member.

7. TIPPING

The word *tip* is an acronym for the phrase, "to insure promptness," and as a tour manager you want promptness and good service for your tour and every member of the group. The practice of tipping is still the only way to insure this. Make good and prudent use of it. It is an essential component of the travel business, even in countries that officially frown on it. Money soothes many bruises.

All tour companies have a basic tipping policy. Familiarize yourself with the policy of the particular company for which you are working. Know what gratuities are included in the tour package, and review them with the clients at the orientation meeting.

Gratuities Included in the Tour

Most tour packages include gratuities for baggage handling in and out of hotels. They also include 15 percent of the cost of all meals included in the tour and gratuities for hotel doormen, bell captains, and maîtres d'hôtel. The gratuities are paid in one of three ways: by adding it to the master bill; by a voucher issued by the company; in cash.

Hotel and restaurant employees are very conscious of tips and check all tours to make sure they are paid. Unfortunately, gratuities given to supervisory personnel are not always distributed among other employees. If this happens at a facility you visit on a regular basis, the employees will soon let you know about it. Make it your policy to hand the gratuity to the management in full view of an employee representative.

"Escorts" sometimes conveniently "forget" to leave gratuities, a practice called "stiffing" in the trade, and this may affect the quality of the service received by subsequent tours. "Forgotten" tips are most often those that are to be paid in cash. Sometimes, because of a problem like a late departure, a tour manager will inadvertently overlook leaving a gratuity. Should this happen on one of your tours, call the hotel or restaurant at your next stop, apologize for the error, and mail the money by check or money order at once. Hotel and restaurant employees do have blacklists of tours and escorts. Do not allow your name to appear on them.

There are times when special tips are in order. A client may have been assigned an unsatisfactory room, or he may have been downgraded on a train. If the hotel clerk or train conductor is able to rectify the matter, he deserves an extra gratuity. When your tour arrives at a hotel at a very busy check-in time, an extra gratuity to the bellhops will normally get your tour luggage "A" priority. Whenever these extra outlays are required, note them on your tour report and expense account. These are legitimate expenses, necessary to create good will and make for smooth operations.

An extra gratuity is sometimes called for when you use the services of a local sight-seeing guide or when you require a chartered bus. Your employer will normally provide funds for these services, but if your local guide or bus driver does a really outstanding job, extra consideration is very much in order. If it is not contrary to your company's policy, you can give such extra tips out of your expense account and explain the outlay in your tour report. Otherwise, you might point out to your clients at the information meeting that the tour price includes the basic gratuity for guides and drivers but that individuals may show their own expressions of gratitude to those who provide exceptional service. Greyhound World Tours gives this advice to its tour managers:

> *Sightseeing tipping schedule will be supplied for each tour.* The Escort cannot urge or force members to contribute a group tip for guides and/or sightseeing drivers. *But he can remind* members that everyday courtesy is very much in order, and that a personal thanks from members to guides and drivers should be given at the conclusion of each day's activities. There are many members who never thank a guide or driver, and who walk past them as if they were wooden statues. We do not ask that he discourage his tour members from tipping if they choose to do so.[17]

TIPPING GUIDE FOR TRAVELERS

Prepared by

Travel Associates Ltd.   Box 506   Jasper, Alberta, Canada

The word "TIP" stands for "to insure promptness" and had its origin at a restaurant in London, England. The practice of tipping for service has become a world wide custom and in North America, most salaries in the travel industry are based upon the fact that employees do receive tips. Even the Income Tax people assume this fact and taxes are withheld on that basis.

The purpose of this guide is to give the traveler an idea of what the usual amount of a tip should be. Tipping is a personal thing and it should be given for *good* service. It should always be given personally to the person that renders the service if possible. This encourages the receiver to continue to give good service. If the service is *poor,* a lesser amount should be given and a comment made. If you get a waiter or guide that gives you *excellent* service, the amount may be increased and presented with proper comment.

Meals—15% of total bill
Wine Steward or bartender—15% of total bill
Chambermaids—75¢ per person per night
Porters—35¢ per average bag (50¢ for extremely large ones)
Sightseeing Guides—50¢ per person for ½ day, 1.00 for full day
Taxis—15% of meter reading

On tours, check to see what tips are included in the tour price. Usually, porterage and sightseeing tips are included as are the meal gratuities that are part of the package.

If the tour has the same director and driver throughout the tour:

Driver—$5.00 per week per person
Director—$1.00 per day per person

If the tour uses different means of transportation or has different drivers, the gratuity is usually included in the tour price. Sometimes drivers will do more than is expected on the itinerary or do an outstanding job on sidetrips. In such cases, a special gratuity would be in order. If in doubt, consult the tour director. Again, such a special gratuity should be an individual thing and not just an envelope from the group.

Figure 6. Tipping Guide

Client Tipping

At the orientation meeting, outline the tips included in the tour and the special tips outlined above, and then list those the client is expected to pay himself. These are usually tips to chambermaids (.75–$1.00 per room per night), waiters or waitresses for meals not included in the tour (15 percent of bill), wine stewards (15 percent of bill), bellhops for delivery service (.35). Many companies issue a tipping guide for their clients.

Withholding Gratuities

Learn now that tipping is a way of life in the travel business. Proper tipping should insure good service, but it is not guaranteed. On occasion you will get poor or slow service despite generous handouts. If that should happen, the threat of withholding the gratuity may work wonders. But investigate first; the problem may be beyond the control of the waitress or bellhop. Management may be at fault. Speak to the maître d', the bell captain, or the management. Express your dissatisfaction firmly but politely. Give those involved the opportunity to save face.

Rudeness or absolute discourtesy should never be tolerated. When confronted with such a situation, speak to the person in charge and ask that someone else handle the service. If this is impossible, withhold the gratuity due that individual only. Never penalize an entire staff for the poor service of one incompetent person.

Note in your tour report any incident which led to your withholding a gratuity, and show the adjusted amount on your expense account. Advise your clients that you were aware of the poor service to which they were subjected, and inform them of the action you took.

8. LUGGAGE

Handling luggage is a major tourist worry that is eliminated on an escorted tour. It is a service that the tour members expect and appreciate. It is up to the tour manager to see that the clients' luggage is where it is supposed to be at all times. In the following paragraphs, we will outline a procedure for obtaining the luggage count at the departure site and wherever new people join the tour.

All tour companies have limits on the number of suitcases, the types of luggage, and in some cases the weight of the luggage that clients may carry. One company states:

> Porterage charges are included in the rates for one normal-sized piece of luggage on Carefree [first class] and for two pieces of luggage on Priceless [deluxe] per person. Garment bags and car sacks cannot be carried. Amexco is not responsible for loss, theft of or damage to your belongings. For that reason baggage insurance is strongly recommended and available at nominal rates. Ask us or your travel agent. Airline regulations allow you to have 44 pounds of luggage. Anything over that weight is subject to the airline's excess baggage charge.[18]

Some companies strictly enforce their luggage regulations; others do not. Know your company's policy and act accordingly.

If a client insists upon carrying an extra piece of luggage or one not in conformity with company policy, that luggage becomes the responsibility of that client. On most tours, however, it may be easier for you to add it to your count and collect any extra gratuities and similar costs from the client. Methods of dealing with excess-weight luggage charges are dealt with in a later section.

Tour companies issue distinctive luggage tags. Since most of these are made of cardboard, some will be ripped or lost. The remedy: always carry some extras, and replace the originals when necessary. All clients should also have tags showing their names and addresses. This is required by all public carriers.

Always carry with you a felt-tipped marker or crayon, and put a number on each tag. Number the bags consecutively as people check in at the beginning of the tour. Add numbers as new bags are added at the places where additional people join the tour. If your company permits garment bags, leave the first five numbers (1–5) open for them, as they have a tendency to be misplaced. If you do not get five garment bags, you can always assign the unused numbers to the last person who checks in or use them for your own luggage. When the numbers have been assigned, memorize the count as quickly as possible.

Sometimes, a couple will begin a tour with one suitcase but, as they acquire souvenirs and other items, buy another, without apprising you of the fact (remember, they were given two luggage tags by the company). Consequently, you may check out of a hotel with the right luggage count but arrive in Rome to find that Mrs. So-and-So's suitcase is sitting at the hotel in London. This can happen when a client neglects to call additional luggage to your attention. The bellhops will pick up the same number of bags they checked in, your count will tally both at the hotel and at the airports, but Mrs. So-and-So will blame you. You can avoid this situation by telling people at the orientation meeting to advise you if they add a suitcase. Place the responsibility on the group members as early as possible.

Most tour companies encourage clients to purchase baggage insurance because they do not accept responsibility for luggage that has been lost or damaged. The hotel or carrier should be notified at once of any lost or damaged luggage. Offer your client assistance in filling out the necessary forms, and ascertain whether the hotel or carrier will issue the client enough funds for needed toilet articles and at least a change of clothing if his luggage has been lost. Leave your itinerary with the hotel management or the carrier representative, and make sure you follow up to find out whether or not the luggage has been located. In all cases, your tour company must be apprised of the situation and the action you took.

9. CLERICAL WORK

All tour managers are required by their companies to keep extensive records and to file periodic reports. While these vary in size and scope from one tour company to another, they all follow a general pattern. They usually include:

1. Daily report sheet
2. Tour manager's time sheet
3. Report of missed services
4. Expense account report
5. Accident report
6. Passenger tour evaluation sheet
7. Vouchers for services rendered

The Daily Report Sheet

The daily report sheet is an important matter that needs your complete attention.

This sheet will look very much like your own information log. On the top of the page, you will note a space for the name (or number) of the tour and the departure data, plus the day of the week and the date. On subsequent lines, you will record the hotel where you will be staying that night, and evaluate the quality of each service provided. Some companies require you to spell out these evaluations in detail, others issue checklists with space for comments. A few companies list specific items to evaluate in each category (e.g., Hotel: wake-up calls, luggage pickup, breakfast service, etc. See Figure 8).

Filling out this form is one of the most important services you will render as far as the suppliers are concerned. Your evaluation helps the company that employed you to decide if that hotel or that restaurant or that sight-seeing company should be used again. The suppliers know this. They know that each courtesy, each favor, is reported. When "problems" arise, you can use this form to obtain the services for which your company contracted and for which your clients ultimately paid. If there is a problem, make note of it. For example, if a restaurant manager apologizes

68

Pyramid Travel Service
357 Main Street
Anytown, US

Escort's Daily Report

Tour Name: _____ Escort's Name: _____
Departure Date: _____ Day Number: _____
From: _____ To: _____

Hotels, Meals, & Other Stops	Rating	Comments	Time
_____	_____	_____	Depart: _____
_____		_____	
_____		_____	
_____	_____	_____	Arrive: _____
_____		_____	
_____		_____	
_____		_____	Depart: _____
_____	_____	_____	Arrive: _____

Transportation Comments: _____
_____
_____

Additional Remarks: _____
_____
_____

Overall Rating of the Day: _____

Use reverse side of page for additional comments.

Figure 7. Escort's Daily Report

TOUR CONDUCTOR'S DAILY REPORT CHECK LIST

TERMINAL FACILITIES

(A) Personnel—Courtesy, Cooperation, Etc.
(B) Baggage Handling.
(C) Announcements Designating Gate Numbers, Departure Time, Etc.
(D) Proper Direction of Passengers to Tour Bus.

BUS AND EQUIPMENT

(A) General Overall Mechanical Condition.
(B) Appearance—Both Interior and Exterior.
(C) Proper Mechanical Operating of the Air Conditioning, Ventilation and Heating System.

DRIVERS

(A) General Appearance.
(B) Attitude Towards Passengers.
(C) Cooperation with Tour Conductor.
(D) General Operation of Tour Coach and Overall Performance.

REST AND MEAL STOP FACILITIES

(A) Overall Cleanliness.
(B) Lavatory Facilities—Adequate Towels, Soap, Etc.
(C) Personnel and Service.
(D) Cooperation of Local Manager.

HOTELS

(A) Personnel and General Efficiency.
(B) Quality of Room Assignments—Type of Room—General Appearance and Condition.
(C) Cooperation of Bellboys in Handling of Baggage.
(D) Dining Room, Coffee Shop Facilities, General Range of Prices for Meals, Courtesy of Waitresses Towards the Group, Attitude Toward Your Greyhound Tour Group, Promptness of Service, Etc.
(E) Farewell Dinner.

SIGHTSEEING TRIPS AND OTHER ATTRACTIONS

(A) Condition of Sightseeing Equipment.
(B) Attitude, Cooperation, Friendliness of Personnel.
(C) General Efficiency of Operation.

Figure 8. Tour Conductor's Daily Report Check List

for slow service by explaining that only one of his waitresses appeared for work, accept his apology and state the exact problem in your report. The company will quickly come to know if this story is used as a cover for poor service every time a tour stops at this restaurant. Conversely, if the service rendered was better than one would expect, include that fact in your report.

There is a tour manager's "grapevine." Bad news travels fast. Should a certain hotel or attraction be having problems, you will probably soon hear about it. Some time ago, one of North America's most famous resort hotels was modernizing its kitchen. As a result, the service was slow, particularly at the dinner hour. By advising the clients of the situation and by making an extra "coffee stop" before arriving at the hotel, the managers avoided having hungry people on their hands. Get into the habit of writing up incidents, and explain how you handled the situation.

Tour Manager's Time Sheet

Most tour companies pay a per diem salary; some pay on an hourly basis. Some provincial or state labor departments require companies to keep hourly records even on managers receiving a per diem salary. All time sheets follow the same design. At the top, there is a place for your name and that of the tour, as well as the departure date. In the left-hand column you will find the dates of the tour, and in the next column the starting time. This is followed by a column for finishing time, another for total time, and finally a space for remarks. It is best to use the twenty-four-hour clock in recording your times, and do not forget the gain or loss when you change time zones. Note the time-zone change in the remarks column.

Most escorts are confused about what to include in their count of hours worked. The rule is a simple one: you count your time from the minute you begin work in the morning until you complete your paperwork in the evening. In a later chapter, we will suggest that you begin your day by stopping at the cashier's desk of the hotel where you are staying and having the cashier prepare your bill while you are having breakfast. That stop at the cashier's

Globus Tours Ltd.

Tour Director's Time Sheet

Name _____ Tour _____ Departure _____

Date	Start	Finish	Total	Remarks
1				
2				
3				
4				
5				
6				
7				
8				
9				
10				
11				
12				
13				
14				
15				
16				
17				
18				
19				
20				
21				
22				
23				
24				
25				
26				
27				
28				
29				
30				
31				

Total Hours _____
Signature _____

Figure 9. Tour Director's Time Sheet

wicket begins your working day. If dinner is included in the tour, you continue to count until you have eaten, returned to your room, and completed your last form. Each company has its own rules about free half days and free full days. As a general rule, on a full free day, you are given eight hours' working credit since you are not at home.

If your day extends beyond what is listed on the itinerary, or an emergency occurs during the night, add those extra hours to your count and explain them sufficiently in the remarks column; for example, "flight delayed two hours at O'Hare Airport," or "Mrs. Smith ill during the night." You do not have to elaborate here; your daily report sheet is the place for a full explanation of the incident.

Report of Missed Services

The itinerary tells the client exactly what services will be rendered on the tour. Almost every itinerary includes a clause giving the company the right to change it, but the report of missed services is not concerned with company changes. This report deals with changes on the tour caused by mechanical failure, strikes, acts of God, and other situations not anticipated by the company. For example, if the itinerary calls for a cable car ride to the top of a mountain and you find that the car will not run due to mechanical failure, this should be counted as a missed service. The experienced tour manager should know of an equivalent attraction that could be substituted. If the cost is the same or less, the company will usually cooperate with you and approve your switch.

Some of the tour members may decide not to take advantage of side trips included in the tour, such as a city sight-seeing tour. Your report should give the names of those who do not participate and their reasons for nonattendance. New escorts are surprised at the number of people who "opt out" of included items and events, some because they have been there before, others because they want to shop or write cards. The usual reason, however, is that they want to rest. Touring is a chore to many, no matter how pleasant you try to make it.

Downgrading, giving a client something of less value than he paid for, should also be recorded. A client is entitled to everything he was promised. In some of the older resort hotels there are few "single" rooms available, and if you have a large number of single travelers on your tour, some may have to share a room. When this happens, record the names of the people involved, the name of the hotel, and the number of nights they were doubled up.

The best rule to follow is to record the name of any client who does not get or does not take advantage of everything he is supposed to have, according to the itinerary. Any change made by the company prior to the departure of the tour should be discussed at the orientation meeting and need not be included on this report.

Expense Account Report

The form for reporting expenses has so many variations from company to company that it is quite impossible to give more than very basic information here. There are two types. One is a daily entry page, arranged by general categories, for example, admissions, gratuities, telephone, and so on. The amount spent on each item is entered and the columns subtotaled. At the end of the page all subtotals are tallied and deducted from the opening amount. The other type is an actual day-by-day estimate of expenses as outlined in the itinerary. On this type of expense record you enter the actual amount. There is space for an explanation of any changes.

Keep your expense account report up to the minute (record as you spend), and at the end of the day recheck your figures and balance with your expense fund before you retire. It is easier to rectify a mistake while it is fresh in your mind than to try to reconstruct it a week later. As treasurer, you are entrusted with a great responsibility. Keep that trust and earn the respect of those with whom you work.

Accident Report

The accident report should be completed whenever anyone (including yourself) sustains an accident. If the injury occurs at a hotel, at an attraction, or on a public carrier, the suppliers' accident form should also be completed. Both reports should contain the same basic information. Include as many details as possible, and obtain the names and addresses of witnesses. Also include a report of the accident in your daily report sheet.

Passenger Tour Evaluation Sheet

Passengers' evaluation forms are filled out by the clients. This gives them an opportunity to evaluate the hotels and attractions on the tour and to report on your performance, as well as to make comments of a general nature. Most companies use forms that are self-sealing, prestamped, and addressed to the company. You should distribute these forms near the conclusion of the tour or at the farewell dinner. Some companies send "welcome home letters," timed to arrive just before the client arrives at his residence, which ask for the same type of information.

The client forms combine with your daily reports to supply the tour operator with a basis for decisions about changes in the future itineraries.

Vouchers

Most tour operators work on a voucher payment system with their suppliers. Before the tour starts, you will be supplied with one voucher for each service included on the itinerary. In addition, you will usually receive a few blank vouchers to be used in handling any emergencies that may arise on the tour. If you do not receive these extra vouchers, ask for some. No trip is free of emergencies, and you should be prepared for them.

The individual voucher has space for the name, address, and phone number of the supplier of service and the item to be supplied. A hotel voucher, for example, might read: "For twenty (20) twin rooms, five (5) singles, baggage in and out, and continental breakfast."

Verify the count on the voucher with your list of clients. If someone joins the tour en route, be sure that that person is included in the voucher count from the pickup point. If he is

Date _____

To: From:

_____   Acme Travel Ltd.

_____   387 Avenue Road

_____   Toronto, Ontario

Attn: _____   M3H-3H9

Phone: _____   416-555-3560

                                           Attn: _____

Tour # _____ Number of Passengers _____ plus escort

Date of Arrival _____ Time _____Via _____

Date of Departure _____ Time _____Via _____

Our Requirements:

Rooms: _____ Singles   For _____ nights

              _____ Twins   _____ Bags in

              _____ Triples   _____ Bags out

              _____ Quads

              _____ Escort

Meals: _____ Breakfasts   Type _____

              _____ Lunches   _____

              _____ Dinners   _____

Other Services: _____

_____

_____

_____

Our Tour Director will present you with a signed carbon copy of this order
which will serve as a *voucher*. Please show the billing breakdown on the reverse side of the carbon copy.

Figure 10. Voucher

not, call all of the hotels, add him to the list they already have, and when you make your reconfirmation calls be sure that the correction has been made. Otherwise you will have a complaining, unhappy client on your hands.

When a service has been completed, you should obtain a copy of the bill and write the amount on the voucher before giving the supplier his copy. It often happens that the breakfast charges or the baggage-out costs will not coincide with the cashier's amount when the master bill is presented to you. Note these omissions on the voucher as well as the total rendered, so the tour company's bookkeeper will know that the master bill you signed was not the final one.

Some companies' vouchers come attached to a carbon copy, which later becomes a part of your daily report.

To the tour escort who is just beginning, this mass of reports may seem confusing and extremely time-consuming. Some of them may seem unnecessary. Two reports may ask for the same information in a different way. Yet all are important to the company's operation and should be filled out daily. Most of the escorts' manuals issued by the tour operators have detailed instructions as well as sample forms. As you become familiar with them, they will take less time to complete. If there is anything you do not understand, check the manual. If still in doubt, seek the help of another tour manager. Even if that manager has never worked for your employer, he will be able to help you, since the form will be similar to those he must complete for his own company. Where there is no manager available, you should call headquarters.

10. SPECIAL EVENTS REQUIRING SPECIAL PREPARATIONS

While every day of every tour should be treated as a special occasion for every member of the tour, there are some days that are more special than others. Two of these are particularly stressed by the companies in their tour advertising. The first is the day when the welcome cocktail party and/or dinner is scheduled. Emphasizing the social side of its tours, one company's brochure points out that "Introductions [of tour members] will be made over dinner this evening."[19] The other event stressed by the companies is the final dinner of the tour, called by one operator "The Gala Finale Dinner Party."[20]

Many people treat themselves to tours or receive them as gifts for a birthday, anniversary, or other important personal event, and the tour director should see that these special dates are observed in some special way. The entire group may often be involved in these festivities. When a tour operates during the holiday season or on a national holiday, this naturally deserves some special attention. If informed, your hotel will help you arrange some recognition of events such as these, which may become outstanding highlights of the trip.

The Welcome Party

The practice of holding some type of "welcome" gathering, while "standard operating procedure" on deluxe tours and some first class tours, is questioned by some tour operators. Many operators never schedule any sort of Get-Acquainted affair. The operators who always make a Welcoming event a part of the tour hold that "The purpose of the Welcome Party is for the tour members to get acquainted with each other and develop the sense of 'group.' It should also establish the mood of the trip as being 'fun' and relaxation with friends."[21] Operators who do not hold such events assert that the cost overrides the benefits received.

Another debatable aspect of the Welcome Party is its timing. The itinerary of the full tour should be considered; the welcome party need not automatically take place on the first day. On many tours, the first day is usually a long travel day, and the clients were probably up early in the morning and busy making the tour connection. It is most likely that they slept very little the night before, due to either excitement and anticipation of the trip or last-minute packing or both. A person who is tired and perhaps suffering from jet lag is not really in a party mood. Considering these possibilities, it is wiser to schedule the party for the second night. By then, the clients have developed a festive routine. They already recognize some of the other tour members by sight and have established a speaking acquaintance with others. More importantly, you have established yourself as their leader. A party is then in order, and they will welcome it. You should make the most of it.

If the first day is a short one, or if the tour begins with an afternoon check-in at a hotel, the party could be held that night. There is already a festive spirit, and the clients will enjoy it. They will want it to be a success, and that helps.

Regardless of the day on which it is held, make sure that the clients have had sufficient time to relax, and allow enough time for them to get properly dressed for the party. The party should be held in a private room or in a reserved section of a larger hall, and the tour manager should be in the room at least one half hour before the party begins to make certain that all is in readiness. Wherever possible, make name tags available for your group. It is best to have each client fill out his own, since some people prefer to be called by nicknames, and the manager does not always know this. Encourage informality in name tagging; it makes for friendship. At a cocktail party, avoid table seating. Have plenty of room for your people, and make sure they mingle and circulate. At a dinner, arrange the seating in a circle, if possible, so that everyone can see each other and become better acquainted.

As manager, you are the official host and toastmaster at the party. When the group is assembled, welcome them on behalf of the company and yourself. If it is the second night of the tour, a few remarks are in order about what a good group they are. A compliment goes a long way. Thank them for their cooperation, encourage them to have a good time, and then see that they do enjoy themselves. Be helpful, cheerful, polite, and available, and mingle well.

The Farewell Dinner

The farewell dinner is usually scheduled for the last evening of the tour, and like the welcome dinner it calls for special preparation. This dinner, too, should be held in a private room, if possible. If this cannot be arranged, use a corner of a large room. Seating should be banquet style.

Be in the room early to see that everything is ready for the guests. Greet each person as he enters, and if cocktails are included see that each person is served his favorite drink. When all have arrived, toast the group and tell them how happy you are that they were with you. Be polite and congenial.

The farewell dinner serves many purposes, the main ones being:

1. to end the tour on a happy note even if there were some difficulties along the way
2. to promote other possible tours that the company operates
3. to give the tour members and opportunity to express their gratitude to you for the job you have done

After cocktails or, if they are not included, when all the members of the group have arrived, the group should be seated and the appetizer and/or soup served. Make arrangements for a ten-minute delay in serving the main course, and use the time to express your thanks to the group for taking the tour. Review quickly the high points of the tour as well as some of the funny incidents. Remind the group that you will be with them until the end of the tour and that you hope to have the privilege of escorting them on another of the company's tours.

Client Occasions

It is a common occurrence for one of the tour members to celebrate a birthday or for a couple to observe a wedding anniversary while on tour. Most tour companies or travel agents attempt to obtain this information in advance; however, the tour manager will often be the first to discover these events. Tour companies generally have some policy governing the method of observing these special days. Usually the tour manager sends a bottle of wine and a congratulatory note, at dinnertime, to the table of the person or couple celebrating, but flowers or some other gift may be substituted. The idea is not to let the event pass without recognition on your part.

Often, people do not wish to have such occasions celebrated in public. They do not want to draw the attention of the entire group; they prefer to keep their celebrations private. For that reason, it is wise to first approach the person's traveling companion for advice before planning the event. If the person is traveling alone, try to ascertain his feelings on the subject without letting your purpose become too obvious. In all cases, the observance of a special occasion should be a pleasant surprise and handled with discretion and dignity.

Holidays

A celebration for the entire group should be carefully planned if a major holiday occurs during the tour. A special festival dinner with wine is a standing policy with most tour companies, and they will have made the arrangements beforehand. A North American tour will look forward to a turkey dinner with all of the trimmings on Thanksgiving and Christmas and a cocktail party on New Year's Eve. If the company somehow overlooked these arrangements, you must provide them. People look forward to these events and expect them. Seeing that they are not disappointed is part of being a generous and affable host.

Take particular notice of national holidays like Canada Day and Independence Day, particularly if the tour is outside of the mother country. Observe them in some special way that will emphasize the importance of the holidays. If you have foreign nationals aboard and learn that their national holiday occurs during the period of the tour, send some wine or cocktails to their tables during dinner that evening.

Much of the tour manager's work, like the teacher's preparation work is done out of sight of the clients. While routine and time-consuming, it is just as important as the pretour preparation and "on camera" work and insures the smooth operation of the tour. When your clients realize that you are working quietly for them behind the scenes, your leadership role will be enhanced. People on tour wish to be relaxed, and the consciousness of being in good hands and under responsible care will insure their peace of mind.

QUESTIONS FOR DISCUSSION

1. What are the major sources of information used by a tour manager in preparing for a tour?
2. In preparing to escort a tour, what types of information should the escort seek?
3. What is the purpose of the tour manager's information log? What types of information should it contain?
4. How is it possible to live out of one suitcase for an extended period of time?
5. Discuss the procedures used in reconfirmation calls.
6. What procedures should be followed for speedy clearance at immigration?
7. How can the escort avoid problems during a customs clearance abroad? Returning home?
8. What are some techniques that can be employed to assist clients with the problems associated with foreign exchange?
9. A tour manager can use tipping to improve or ruin a tour. How is this possible?
10. What is the importance of the luggage count?
11. What are some of the uses, by companies, of the tour manager's daily report?
12. What are some of the real and imagined problems that a single traveler encounters, and how can the tour manager overcome them?
13. What are considered special occasions on tours, and what preparations are made for celebrating these occasions?

NOTES

1. This point was well made in "Diary of a Tour Escort," *Travel Weekly,* Aug. 1, 1974, which was written by staff columnist Nadine Goodwin, who posed as a tour escort in training.
2. For a complete list of these offices, see: *Discover America Package Tour Handbook* (Washington, D.C.: Discover America Travel Institute, 1972).
3. Mobil Oil Co., *Mobil Travel Guide;* published for seven regions by Rand McNally, annually.
4. Kevin M. Cahill, *Medical Advice for the Traveler* (New York: Holt, Rinehart and Winston, 1970), p. 61.
5. Ibid.
6. For more detailed information on man-made fibers, see: Man-Made Producers Association, *Guide to Man-Made Fibers;* published by the association, Washington, D.C., 1973. J.C. Penney Co., *Modern Fibers and Fabrics* (New York, n.d.); the chart on p. 23 is particularly useful.
7. For more details on packing, see: Abby Rand, *How to Get to Europe and Have a Wonderful Time* (New York: Charles Scribner's Sons, 1974), pp. 127-130.
8. Four Winds Tours, *General Briefing Outline for Tour Directors,* 1975, p. 5.
9. Told to the author by a client at Big Chief Mountain Crossing (between Alberta and Montana), summer 1975.
10. Pan American World Airways, *The Pan American Immigration Guide,* a loose-leaf album filed by county and containing all of the current immigration regulations. This book is constantly updated and is available at Pan American ticket offices and at appointed agencies.
11. Four Winds Tours, *General Tour Managers Manual,* 1975, p. 7.
12. Department of the Treasury, U.S. Customs Service, *Know Before You Go* (Washington, D.C.: Government Printing Office); constantly revised.
13. Revenue Canada, Customs and Excise, *I Declare (Je déclare)* (Ottawa: Ashton Potter, Ltd.); constantly revised.
14. Letter to the author from Ms. C.Y. Thibodeau, International Traffic Division, Headquarters Operations, Revenue Canada, Customs and Excise, Ottawa, June 1975.
15. Section 148.33, Customs Regulations, Articles Acquired Abroad.
16. Section 148.63, Customs Regulations, Crew Exemption.
17. Greyhound World Tours, Inc., *Escort's Training Manual,* p. 2.
18. Amexco, *American Express to Europe, 1976,* p. 145.
19. Trans World Airlines, *TWA Getaway Europe, 1976,* p. 116.
20. Maupintours, *Europe, 1975,* p. 7.
21. Remarks by the author at the annual meeting of the Four Winds Tour Directors, New York, Apr. 1975.

PART 4

Basic Tour Management Procedure

Time and time again, our clients write or call us: "You made us feel so special." Such enthusiastic and grateful response is the result of careful attention to even smallest details . . . [by] extraordinary tour conductors who skillfully escort each tour with professional competence, consideration, and yes, "tender loving care."
Olsen Tours brochure

11. THE FIRST DAY

Once you have completed your pretour preparations, selected and packed your wardrobe, stopped at the tour company office for the tickets and any last-minute instructions, you are ready to begin the actual job of leading a tour. For you, as for your clients, the first day is usually the most difficult one. Even if you have had years of experience, the first day means meeting a new group to whom you must prove your competence. For the clients, the first day is the beginning of a new experience. How true it is that first impressions are lasting ones. Your behavior, appearance, and poise on this first day will create an impact that will last for the entire tour. "Always be better dressed than your tour members on the first leg of the journey. Dress at your best; gentlemen should always wear a jacket and tie. Ladies should wear a dress."[1]

The Departure

You should arrive at the tour departure site, which might be an airport, a bus station, a railway terminal, or a hotel lobby, at least an hour before the scheduled check-in time. Learn the locations of the rest rooms, the coffee shop, and, for tours going overseas, the duty-free shops. Most tour companies have special signs and tables at a departure site. See to it that they are properly set up, dusted clean, and ready. Arrange to have a dolly near the table to facilitate carrying the tour members' luggage. Have your list of clients in view as well as an additional supply of luggage tags in case a client has forgotten them. Check your list of clients carefully to determine if some are joining en route. Tours have sometimes been held up waiting for people who were not supposed to be at the departure. Waiting for nobody can be a distasteful experience, and people react unhappily to it.

Now you are ready to greet the members of the tour. As they arrive, introduce yourself, check baggage tags, and begin a running count of the luggage. Make the procedure orderly and efficient. Do not appear to be too preoccupied with these details, yet attend to them with meticulous care and attention. If you are nervous, disturbed, or unhappy, your mood will infect the entire group.

When traveling by train or ship, you must "space" the luggage. Next to each client's name on the tour list, mark the car and compartment number or stateroom number assigned to that person. As you accept each piece of luggage, mark this number on the tag and inform the client of the location of his accommodations. One good way to do this is to mark it on his copy of the tour membership list provided by most tours.

When traveling by air, try to have the airline set aside a block of seats in advance, some in the smoking compartment and some for nonsmoking members of your group. If this cannot be done, have your client select his own seat on the plane.

Remember that there are limits on luggage for overseas air travel. Prior to June 1, 1977, the limit was calculated by weight, but now size is the determining factor in transatlantic air travel. Two pieces of luggage are permitted for each air traveler in addition to a small "carry-on" bag. For a person flying first class, each bag may have a maximum dimension of 62 inches (158 cm). For economy class travelers (the class used by most tours), the total dimensions of both bags must not exceed 106 inches (270 cm), and neither bag may exceed 62 inches (158 cm).

One airline agent says he does not use a tape measure on each piece of luggage; "I get to know by looking whose luggage is within the regulations and whose is not." The owner of a luggage shop catering to overseas travelers told me: "To meet the new regulations, I suggest a 29-inch suitcase, which is sometimes called an overseas bag, and a 21-inch 'carry-on,' or a combination of 26-inch and 24-inch suitcases. It is always better to specify dimensions, rather than terms such as 'two- or three-suiter,' as the actual sizes may vary from manufacturer to manufacturer."[2] Carry-on luggage is limited to 45 inches (115 cm) in all classes, and must fit beneath one aircraft seat. Normally the client must pay excess baggage charges directly to the airline.

The free baggage allowances are different between European countries. British Airways states: "Generally speaking, if your luggage meets the regulations . . . for travel to and from the United States and does not weigh over 30 kilos (66 lbs.) for first class travel or 20 kilos (44 lbs.) for economy class travel, you can be confident you are within allowances applicable for most travel world-wide.''[3]

Keep all luggage tickets in your possession, and be sure the total number of tickets matches the luggage count.

On overseas departures, it is necessary to check your clients' documentation—passports, visas—to insure that all is in order. It is prudent to note on your passenger list, beside each person's name, the country, number, and date of issue of the individual's passport. If a passport is lost, this information will speed up the reissue process. If there is any doubt about a client's documentation, have it checked immediately by the airline or steamship representative, who will know how to deal with any problems. After checking in a client and taking care of his luggage, tell him where to find the rest rooms, gift shops, and so on, and when to be back at the table for boarding with the group. As new clients arrive while others are still at the table, take time to introduce them to each other. This makes for congeniality.

Any clients who have not arrived by the end of the check-in time should be paged over the public address system. Airports and terminals are big places; people get lost easily there. You must make an extra effort to contact any tour member who is lost and let him know exactly where you are located. Notify the company of any "no shows" (a term used to designate people who are supposed to be on the tour but have not checked in before departure time). Most companies have a policy that you and their office are expected to follow in the event that clients do not show up at the appointed place at the appointed hour.

Many airlines, steamships, and trains have preboarding privileges for groups. Advise the carrier's representative when your group is ready for boarding, and if this is the policy, he will have you boarded as a group in advance of everyone else.

En Route

Your first opportunity to meet with the individual members of the group informally will come once the tour is really underway, and this is a good time to begin to learn each person's name. You may begin by saying: "How is everything going?" or "Where is your home city?" Keep each conversation short and, if possible, talk to each one on the tour and give him individual attention. This initial chat, carried out in a friendly manner, will create a good rapport that should help make the trip much more pleasant.

Joinings En Route

Make a note on your tour list of any people who are joining en route, and find out where they are to be met. Advise the group that new people will be joining the tour at a later point.

When the newcomers arrive, give them a special welcome. They may be ill at ease, feeling that they may be encroaching upon a "closed circle" or unsure of their ability to "fit in." If you have already held your orientation meeting, talk with them informally, giving them all the information conveyed at that time. If you are careful to see that they have not missed anything, they will not feel left out.

Be sure to check their luggage, and add it to your list and total count.

The Information Meeting

Soon after the final arrangements were made, the tour company sent each client a memorandum covering all items included in the tour. By the time the tour begins, however, most people have forgotten about it, and you will need to give them the information. The information meeting is important and should never be part of the welcome cocktail party. It should be held before the group arrives at the first hotel, in a place with sufficient privacy to insure your clients' attention.

The best place to hold this meeting on an air tour is on the bus from the airport to the hotel. On shipboard, you can obtain a small meeting room. On a bus tour, you already have the bus. There is no convenient place to meet on a train, particularly if it is an overnight train trip, so you will have to meet with each person or couple on an individual basis.

The following points should be covered at the information meeting:

1. Any changes in the itinerary from that sent to the clients.
2. Tipping: which tips are included in the tour package and which are not. Give guidelines for those that are not.
3. Meal check-signing procedure. Most companies, restaurants, and hotels want the checks to contain: (*a*) the name of the tour company; (*b*) the tour number; (*c*) the client's name; (*d*) the client's room number (in a hotel).
4. Limits on meals, if any.
5. Incidental expenses (because they can be a major problem, they are handled in a separate section).
6. Physical, medical, or dietary problems. Ask that anyone with such a problem contact you privately.
7. Clients' questions.
8. Punctuality. Close by stressing the importance of punctuality; you can never overemphasize this.

Setting the Leadership Role

During this first day, your leadership role will be established. You are new to the group, but if you are friendly, relaxed, and in full control of situations as they arise, your clients will develop a sense of security in your leadership.

Upon debarking from the plane, train, or other means of transportation, see that the members of the group are settled comfortably while you look after their luggage. If immigration and customs must be cleared, know the procedures in order to expedite the clearance.

Finally, in setting your leadership role, "be natural. It is foolish to waste energy being too charming, constantly amusing or attempting to be the authority on all cultural and historic facts. Respect from the group will stem from ability to handle the occasional difficult problems rather than rare wit, humor and charm."[4]

12. HOTEL PROCEDURES

In the course of a normal tour, you will stay at several different hotels. Depending upon the tour, some will be big, inner-city types, some will be resort hotels, and some may be motels. Regardless of the type or location, the basic operation as far as tours are concerned is similar. Your main concern with the hotels' management will be while checking in the tour, again when the tour checks out, and when handling the incidental charges.

Check-In

Most hotels operate on a preregistration system for tour groups. In return, these hotels expect the tour manager to reconfirm the group's reservation no later than twenty-four hours prior to arrival.

When the bus arrives at the hotel, leave the group aboard and go in alone. As you enter the lobby, give the bell captain the luggage count and ask him to have the luggage unloaded while you are registering. Ask him what time he would like the luggage ready for departure in the morning and whether the luggage should be left inside or outside the rooms. After signing the registration form, inquire about mail for the tour members. People on tour sometimes do get mail the first night out; some will receive mail every day of the tour. The desk clerk will hand you a rooming list for your records and give you the individual keys, usually in separate envelopes with the client's name and room number marked on the outside. Arrange with the operator for wake-up calls two hours before your scheduled departure. Now you are ready to face your clients.

When you return to the bus:

1. Give the time of the wake-up call.
2. Give the luggage ready-time, and state whether the luggage should be left inside the room or outside.
3. Announce the departure time and place (usually where the bus is unloaded).

4. Give the dining room hours and any special instructions pertaining to dining.
5. Briefly review the itinerary for the following day, including (*a*) approximate lunch time; (*b*) approximate length of day; (*c*) any special clothing required (e.g., walking shoes).
6. Call the names (beginning with singles), and pass the keys down the aisle.
7. Advise the people that you will be in the lobby for half an hour if they have any problems with their rooms.
8. Wish them an enjoyable evening.

Stand at the bottom step to help people off the bus. Greet each client with a short message, such as "I hope you had a nice day" or "I hope you have a pleasant evening." When the bus has emptied, check for any objects left behind. Should you find any, take them with you. If you will be having a different driver the next day, give today's driver his gratuity.

Upon entering the hotel, check with the bell captain to see if there were any problems with the luggage. People like to get their luggage quickly; see that they do. Once the luggage has been properly distributed, take care of the bellhops' gratuities. See the maître d' to be sure he knows that the tour is in the house and that the dining room should be ready for them.

Remain near the front desk for some time in case your clients need you. If you can identify the owner of any items left on the bus, consult your rooming list and call the client. Articles whose ownership you cannot ascertain should be held in safekeeping until the next time the group is together.

It is usually advisable to be accessible to the group during the dinner hour. This is particularly important during the first days of the tour. Even though you asked if there were any questions on the bus, you will find that most questions are asked privately. If one person has a question about some aspect of the tour, you can be sure that others will have the same question, so make a note of it and give the information to all in the next day's opening remarks.

Check-Out

You should plan to be awakened one half hour earlier than the rest of the tour. On your way to the coffee shop for an early breakfast, ask the cashier to prepare the tour bill and have it ready for you. Following breakfast, complete the check-out procedure with the cashier and present the voucher. If there are any incidental charges, find out to whom they should be charged, and try to see that person privately.

Greet the members of the tour as they arrive in the lobby. When the luggage has been pulled, count the bags together with the bell captain, and have them loaded on the bus. If the bus has not arrived, see that the luggage is stored in a safe place, and count it again when it is loaded. Do not take chances.

At departure time, help the people mount the bus, and then take a head count. If anyone is missing, check the coffee shop and the restaurant as well as his room. Make sure that all keys have been turned in before the bus starts on its journey.

Incidental Charges

The incidental charges that come in with the tour's hotel bill have become such a problem that a few tour companies have attempted to deduct them from the manager's salary. Handled properly, they will never be a problem to you.

Incidental charges consist of phone, valet and laundry, room service, and other nontour costs that guests have charged to their rooms. They are carried on a separate account and presented to the tour manager along with the master tour bill.

At the information meeting, point out that telephone calls made from hotel rooms cost more than those made from the lobby pay phones. In some areas, hotels are permitted to add a service charge for collect and credit card calls. Advise the group to avail themselves of the room phone or any other service of the hotel if they so desire but to be certain to see the cashier on their way to breakfast to clear up the charges.

Hotels do make mistakes. They may charge one of your clients for a service rendered to the room's previous occupant. Check all incidental charges with the people to whom they are charged. If you find that they did not incur the charges, advise the cashier. Usually, the hotel will remove the charge.

One way to protect yourself is to endorse the master tour bill and the voucher with the notation, "all incidental charges cleared," and have a copy of the incidental account stapled to the master bill or your own copy of same and placed with your daily report. Either way, your employer will be aware of what you are doing on your job, and the hotels will appreciate your cooperation.

13. ABOARD THE TOUR BUS

The bus becomes the group's private world. It is here that you develop the feeling of "group." Here, communications can be delivered without attracting the attention of outsiders. Use the bus to impart information and make your daily announcements. In the bus members become acquainted with each other through the rotation of seats, through conversations, group sing-alongs, and other activities. The time spent on the bus should be as pleasant for your clients as the time spent in other tour activities, and you should put your best efforts into planning a meaningful time for all.

While the first and last legs of a tour may utilize another means of transportation, most tour groups spend the greatest part of their time traveling and sight-seeing on a bus. In addition to allowing more flexibility in scheduling the itinerary, a bus is the only "private" means of transportation for a group numbering between twenty-five and forty people.

In the past twenty years, there have been many changes in the design, style, and comfort built into these vehicles, which are now referred to as "deluxe motor coaches" by both North American and European tour operators.[5] In addition to larger, picture-type windows, improved air conditioning, and better suspension system, the modern motor coach in North America contains a rest room.[6]

When luggage is being moved, always arrange to have the bus arrive at the hotel or terminal about half an hour before the scheduled departure time. You can do this when you place your reconfirmation call. When the motor coach arrives, inspect it for cleanliness and make sure that everything is working properly (e.g., check the air conditioning, public address system, paper and towels in the washroom). If everything is not up to standard, report it to the driver. If he is unable to rectify the condition, call the dispatcher supplying the service. Do everything in your power to have every vehicle you use clean in appearance and in tip-top working order.

Sit down with the driver and review the day's itinerary. Ask him if he has any suggestions. If he is a local resident, he may know much that you do not. Asking him for suggestions or comments is also a way of getting him involved in the tour.

After the luggage has been loaded, have the bus brought as close as possible to the hotel exit the tour members will be using, enter the lobby, and escort the members aboard.

Seat Rotation

Almost every tour company requires mandatory seat rotation for each day of the tour. This moving around assures everyone an opportunity to occupy a front seat as well as one over the wheels. There are many ways of rotating seats, but one of the fairest and most useful for group tours is as follows:

1. On the first day, let everyone choose his own seat.
2. During that first ride, announce that seat rotation is company policy.
3. Have the people on the free (nondriver's) side move up two seats (one on long tours) while those on the opposite side move two seats back. Those in the front or rear of the bus move across the aisle.
4. Inform the group that seat rotation will take place twice a day, in the morning and after lunch, unless a move was just a transfer (say, from the hotel to a historic site three miles away); then there would be only one seat change that day.

Then show the people how it works. Using the people in the first seat on the right side (except in right-hand-drive countries), show them that they would move across the aisle and into the second seat behind the driver, the people in the second seat right would move behind the driver, and so forth.

This system of rotation affords the clients additional opportunities to meet and chat with everyone on the tour, as there will always be new people across the aisle. It also gives everyone a view from both sides of the bus.

Smoking On Tour

In the midseventies, both Canadian and U.S. authorities placed restrictions upon where people may smoke in a bus. While these rules do not have to apply to charter service, it is best to see that they are enforced. Most buses hold at least forty-three people, while tours usually are limited to thirty-five; this leaves the back seats empty, and they can be used as a smoking section.

One tour operator, aware of the smoking controversy and the desire of some people to completely avoid smoke-filled air, states that "As a special consideration to vacationers who do not smoke, there will be NO SMOKING DEPARTURES on some of our tours this year. There will be no smoking permitted on the motor coaches or during any group functions."[7]

Activities On the Bus

After posing as a tour guide in training, Nadine Goodwin wrote that "one source of tension centered on how much talking the guide should do and how much the travelers should do among themselves. . . . There were those who wanted to hear every word, 'after all, we're paying for this information,' but others wanted more opportunity to chat among themselves and comment upon what they were seeing."[8] A tour manager must know when to talk and when to stop.

On every tour, certain information must be given out during specific times of the day. At departure, as the bus is leaving the hotel, is the time to cover the following points.

1. Introduction of the driver if he is new to the tour
2. Itinerary for the day
3. Time and place of rest and lunch stops
4. Arrival time at the hotel
5. Any special events

6. General answers to privately asked questions
7. Items left on the bus the previous day

It is then best to leave the microphone and walk through the bus to informally visit with each person. Try to find out during these chats such things as how the members enjoyed the hotel, and note any complaints they may have. These informal talks will give you an opportunity to find out why your clients joined this particular tour. All travelers have fantasies about the places they will be visiting, and if you can discover them you may be able to help your clients' dreams come true.

Tour members want to know something about each country, state, and/or province whose border they cross and each major city through which the tour passes. This information should include such things as population, size, and major industries. Historic spots, particularly those that tour members may have learned about in school, should be discussed at length. People also like to know the major crop(s) of the areas they are passing through. This is the type of information you should research and place in your information log. If someone on your tour desires specific information that would probably not be of general interest to the entire tour, discuss it with him in private.

When the scenery is extremely boring or the weather is inclement, some type of entertainment is in order. People get bored easily. Group sing-alongs are very popular provided that they consist of old favorites familiar to most people on the tour. However, any activity that continues too long loses its effectiveness, so try to plan a singing session that lasts no more than half an hour and ends at a rest, at mealtime, or at another type of stop.

A certain guide, when traveling through monotonous country, conducts a "daily reading" of a popular newspaper column, such as Ann Landers' advice column. After reading each letter, he gives three or four possible answers and then has the people vote on which one was actually printed in the paper.

Bingo boards are supplied by some companies for use on days of extensive travel.

Humor is appreciated by most people; if you tell jokes well, use them where appropriate. All jokes should be in good taste and not insulting to any group or individual.

N.B.: There are two times in the day when you will find that anything you say to the group will be forgotten, misunderstood, or never heard. The first of these is about fifteen minutes after the morning rest stop, and the other is right after lunch. At these times, most members drop off for a little nap. The experienced tour manager knows that and follows the motto, "If you can't beat 'em, join 'em"; he, too, takes his rest.

Rest Stops

Tour managers agree that after riding a bus for two hours and fifteen minutes a rest stop is always in order, even if the motor coach is equipped with a rest room. Many tour members do not feel comfortable using the rest room on the bus, and many more want an opportunity to "stretch their legs." Finding places to stop on major highways is seldom a problem, as restaurants and coffee shops along these roads usually have large rest rooms. A rest stop on a side road or "scenic route," however, can be as time-consuming as eating lunch. If there is a preponderance of one sex on the tour, it will save time if you can arrange for your group to use both rest rooms, regardless of sex. If there are no other groups at the stop, the management will usually cooperate.

Allot a reasonable amount of time for a rest stop in relation to the day's itinerary. If lunch will be earlier or later than is usual, emphasize this fact before unloading the bus so your clients will know whether or not to order a snack.

Meal Stops

Your reconfirmation call to a restaurant should indicate your approximate time of arrival and the number of people in your tour. When you arrive, see if the staff is ready for you before you unload the bus. Advise the tour members that service will always be faster if they sit down and place their orders first and then use the rest rooms or look for postcards while the food is being prepared.

Should the restaurant you are using have a reputation for slow service, advise the group of this beforehand. Allow a reasonable time for eating, and if someone is not at the gathering spot at the appointed time, find out why he is delayed.

Picture Stops

Tourists and cameras go together like bread and butter. The motto of Parks Canada is, "Leave nothing but your footprints, take nothing but your pictures." Lundberg points out that "the wise traveler exploits his trip while traveling, when newly returned home and for years thereafter."[9] One of the best ways of doing the last is with photographs.

Recognizing the importance of picture-taking to the tourist, some tour companies explicitly recommend that the more experienced photographer bring his exposure meter, light filters, and telephoto lens. Clients should be encouraged to take advantage of every photographic opportunity, and should be allotted sufficient time to do so in a leisurely manner.

A tour manager should be prepared to assist clients who may be using new or unfamiliar equipment. If you are not a photographer, you might ask a camera store operator to show you some basic types of cameras and instruct you in their operation.

If, on tour, a client asks your help with a camera that is unfamiliar to you, ask another member of the tour who appears to be a "shutterbug" for assistance, or visit the camera shop found at most tourist attractions. The personnel are usually happy to help.

Many tourist attractions, such as the Bouchardt Gardens in British Columbia and Disney World in Florida, have set up and marked "picture stops." Point out these service spots on your tour, and mention other places that were particular favorites of other tours.

Evening Announcements

Approximately one half hour before arrival at the hotel where you are to spend the night, you should begin your final announcements of the day. These should include the following: (1) a summary of the day; (2) the next day's itinerary—include information that might influence dress, for example, "We will be doing a lot of walking" or "It will be cool on the lake"; also give the lunch time so people can plan their breakfast accordingly. Then, as you did after the morning announcements, make informal visits through the bus, clearing up any misunderstandings and finding out how the clients enjoyed the day. As you near the hotel, point out places your clients might like to see after dinner.

The Driver and the Tour Manager

"As you might imagine, one of the most important 'on the bus relations' is your relationship with the driver."[10] He is responsible for the safe and smooth operation of the vehicle, while you are responsible for the tour. This should be, and almost always is, a working partnership. As we suggested earlier, go over the itinerary with the driver before you pick up the people. If there is a difference of opinion between the driver and yourself, this is the time to find out. If it is a major difference, say, his refusal to follow the itinerary, you will have time to contact the dispatcher, who will either assign another driver or send a company representative to settle the matter. A situation like this rarely happens. Tour drivers are selected for their competence and pleasant personalities and often make valid suggestions that will aid the tour.

You have a responsibility to assist the driver in maintaining the safe operation of the bus. Some of the ways you can do this are:

1. Be thoroughly familiar with general safety rules and regulations.
2. Be familiar with the location and use of the first aid kit on each bus.

3. In case of road failure, placing flares, flags or fuses as required by safety regulations.
4. Going for assistance while the driver protects the vehicle and passengers or vice-versa.
5. Assisting the driver in changing tires, installing and removing skid chains, or making minor repairs.
6. Placing of parcels and hand luggage properly in luggage racks to avoid mishaps.
7. Ensuring that windshields and windows are kept clean at all times for better vision.
8. Dismounting when the vehicle approaches a railroad crossing and flagging the driver across the track or doing similar duties when the bus is turning around on a busy highway or entering or leaving a driveway.
9. Seeing that passengers remain seated while coach is in motion and preventing unnecessary conversation or annoyance to the driver.
10. To be on the alert at all times to look out for the general safety of the passengers throughout the entire course of the tour.[11]

14. MEETING GROUP NEEDS

Meals

People on tours, like armies, travel on their stomachs. Good meals en route make up for many minor discomforts and/or "cultural shock."

Escorted tours are divided into two classes with reference to meals: those that include most meals—usually referred to as "all-inclusive tours"—and those that do not include meals. Know which class of tour you are conducting before you begin your pretour preparation. All-inclusive tours usually do not include every dinner in major cities (like Montreal, New York, London, Paris) that are noted for excellent restaurants. A few do not include meals other than breakfast on free days. In your tour information log, note the meals that are not included and prepare a list of restaurants to suggest. Advise the group if reservations are necessary, and point out that it is always wise to call the restaurant in advance, especially if it is well-known. If a large group wishes to go to a particular restaurant as a party, offer to make the call for them. It is very difficult to seat a large group together in the more famous restaurants, but seating at adjoining tables can be arranged if enough advance notice is given.

Always check the times of service in the hotel dining room for meals included in the tour. A client who misses a dinner for which he has paid because you neglected to tell the group that the dining room closed at 8:00 P.M. will be very unhappy, and you and the rest of the group will know about it. If you tour is running late, advise the maître d' of that fact and see if he can arrange to accommodate you.

Meals on all-inclusive tours may be one of three types, and the type should be indicated on your copy of the itinerary and on the voucher. The three types are:

1. A la carte, which means that the client has free choice of the full menu. Some companies limit the choices; know these limitations and explain them to the group.

2. Table d'hôte, which means that a restaurant has a full menu at a set price regardless of selections. This type of menu is usually found at resort hotels. These restaurants generally have surcharges for special items like shrimp cocktail appetizers or the jumbo-size steak. Most companies require their clients who order such items to pay for them in cash before signing the dinner check.

3. Set Menu, which means that all members of the group are served the same thing. This type of service is employed most frequently at a lunch stop or an early breakfast, when only a limited amount of time is available for feeding the group. You may also find a set menu at a specialty restaurant like the Space Needle in Seattle, which can accommodate groups only on this basis. If one of your clients has a dietary provision or limitation, you can usually arrange something for him on the reconfirmation call. Generally, however, if a client wants to depart from the set menu, he has to pay for it himself.

Dietary limitations, incidentally, should be made known to you by the company. If you have missed any, try to find out at the information meeting. Most hotel dining rooms will respect these limitations and try to help, provided they know about them. You should let them know when you place your reconfirmation call. There will be no extra charge. This is another instance in which the basic rule for success is sustained: "The more information you have and pass on when necessary, the smoother the trip will be for the client."

When meals are not included on a tour, be prepared to suggest a number of eating establishments or restaurants with a wide price range. Always include a restaurant where liquor is served, since many people enjoy a cocktail with their meals. Determine if the hotel you are using has both a restaurant and a coffee shop, and learn when each is open. For lunch, try to find a large, cafeteria-style operation with both self-service and waitress service; or stop in a community with a choice of restaurants. A good source of information about restaurants is the bus driver who is taking the group through the area.

If meals are not included in the cost of the tour, you have no right to steer people to eat in any one place. However, if a client has complained about bad food or become ill in a restaurant, whether or not you suggested it, you have a right to warn people about it. Nothing can wreck a schedule faster than a few people suffering intestinal upsets from bad food.

Alcoholic Beverages

Guided tours are composed of many people, with widely varying opinions about alcoholic beverages and their use. You will have clients who are totally opposed to the use of alcohol, and unfortunately, once in a while you will have clients who are addicted to it. A person who has a drinking problem may or may not be a problem to you. If he or she is not upsetting the tour or bothering the other members and is not a public nuisance, then you will not have to address yourself to the problem. You simply ignore it. However, if a drinking person is upsetting the tour or does become a public nuisance, you must take steps to remedy the situation. This topic is dealt with in a later section on the expulsion of a tour member.

Today, even those opposed to the use of alcohol accept the fact that drinking is part of the scene in Western civilization. You as the tour manager must make provisions for those who enjoy social drinking. You should know the location of the duty-free shops at airports and border crossings and the amount of liquor each person is allowed to carry with him. Before you enter a "dry" area or one with Sunday "blue laws," inform the group of this fact. You may also inform the group when you are in a jurisdiction with low taxes on spirits. If you stop at a duty-free shop or any other type of liquor store, try to find something for the nondrinkers as well, so they will not feel you are wasting their time.

Many people enjoy a cocktail or wine with their meals, and provisions should be made for them where possible. Except at the welcome party and the farewell dinner, alcoholic beverages are usually not included in the tour price. When meals are included in the tour, be sure that a client pays for any drinks he orders before he signs his dinner check.

You will probably eat with the group when meals are included in the tour, and the question may arise of what to do when your clients order cocktails and ask you to join them. Some companies forbid the managers to drink while on duty. If it is lunchtime, then the answer must always be no. If there is no rule or it does not apply, then the decision is yours. If you would like a drink and can handle it, accept the offer. If you do not wish to drink, decline the offer. Always express appreciation for the offer of a drink, even if you do not accept it.

Shopping

Shopping, or at least looking, is a favorite pastime of most tourists. As a tour manager, you should know what products a country or region is noted for and where they may be obtained at reasonable (or fair) prices. You should also know the major department stores in the cities where you have free time. It is not advisable to include shopping as part of a day's itinerary, unless you are passing through an area noted for a particular product or bargains that are not available where you will have free time for shopping.

There is a wide difference of opinion within the industry as to the advisability of a tour manager recommending particular stores. This is called "steering" in the trade. If you are familiar with the area and know the stores or if you have had clients tell you about good buys in a particular place, you should pass this information on to your group. Goodwin, in the article she wrote after posing as a tour guide in training, points out that the manager she assisted seemed concerned throughout the trip that passengers might think there was something in it for him when he made a recommendation, but "as he personally was accepted and liked by the clients, for his wide knowledge and charm, no one seemed the least bit suspicious."[12]

The rule is simple: do what is good and right for your clients. If you know of something good, share it. Of course, you never have the right to force a client to visit any particular shop.

Sight-Seeing

Most tour companies employ local sight-seeing companies in major cities, in national parks, and at historic sites to show the clients the important things to be seen there. This practice can save you much time and effort, as you will not have to research those areas in depth. However, you should know something about each place you visit. As you enter the city or park, give some general information and tell the group that a local guide who is more knowledgeable about the area will provide them with specific details.

If the guide seems to know the area well, ask him to suggest restaurants and other places of interest the group might like to visit when his tour is over. Be sure to make notes of his recommendations; someone is sure to ask you later, "What was the name of the seafood restaurant the guide told us about?"

You should always accompany your group on a local tour, not only to learn something yourself but to see that the guide performs the service for which the company contracted. City tours have been known to "drop" a group at a zoo or similar spot for an hour, leaving the members stranded to shift for themselves instead of showing them the sights of the city. Sight-seeing is exactly what it says—seeing sights; visiting interesting places; learning about the country, the people, the history, the customs; and imbibing local color.

After using the same local tour on several trips, you may discover that your clients would prefer some changes in the itinerary (more time at one spot, less at another).

You can try to arrange such changes with the local guide, but do this in advance of the tour. Some companies require all tours to follow a standard route, and your request for a change may have to be cleared through the office before the tour begins.

15. MEETING INDIVIDUAL NEEDS

Escorted tours are tailored with the idea of offering peace of mind, economical travel, and personable companionship. Unfortunately, however, a large part of the public pictures such tours as a group of people wearing badges and doing the same things at the same time, with no allowance made for individual difference in taste. To counter this image of regimentation, Swissair recently ran a full-page advertisement in several leading North American newspapers headed, "How Can a Person as Unique as You Be Happy with a Pre-Packaged Tour?"[13] The story that follows pointed out the wide variety of tours now being offered. Even so, no tour will be composed of people sharing identical interests.

Dr. Samuel Porrath, the founder and director of the Institute for Transportation, Travel, and Tourism at Niagara University, commented that "A good Tour Manager should know how to unlock the locked-in feeling that tour members sometimes get."[14] There are several ways to do this.

Group Identification

When a person makes his final reservations for a particular tour, he receives from the tour operator a distinctive, laminated membership badge and an official flight bag. While some individuals relish this group identification, others do not. Except at the welcome cocktail party, where some form of identification should be encouraged, the traveler should be free to use these items or not, as he pleases. As a tour manager, you must develop the skill of recognizing your tour members on sight. Do not encourage regimentation.

If you distribute room assignments, keys, mail, and so on, on the bus, tour members will be able to enter the hotel lobby as individuals. If, for some reason, you must assemble the tour in a public place, try to find a secluded corner or alcove. Make your people feel that you consider them intelligent, capable travelers; do not treat them like children in a classroom.

Tour members should be free to eat dinner at times of their

own choosing. If some wish to eat together, they will quickly form their own subgroup. When the entire group must eat together, make it a special occasion, a time for socializing.

Make your clients feel that they are a group of friends who just happen to be traveling together, not a herd of cattle being driven to market. Remember that they are human beings, who want to maintain their pride and dignity at all times.

Special Interests

Earlier, we discussed the importance of learning what your clients' special interests are. With this information, you will be in a position to cater to these interests wherever possible. Of course, this should be done discreetly; showing favoritism or inflicting one client's interest on the entire group will incur the antagonism of the others.

You can discuss a client's special interest and its application to the area you are passing through in private discussion. If you know of something of special interest near the route you are taking, you may be able to arrange to make a detour past it or use it as a rest stop.

However, the best way to meet individual differences and interests is in helping clients to plan their free time.

Free Time

Most tours include some half days and/or full days during which no tour activities are scheduled. This free time allows the tour members to rest, have their laundry done, write cards, shop, or follow up on their own particular interests.

You will probably be asked about the laundry situation, so you should know whether the hotel has twenty-four-hour laundry and valet service and whether there is a self-service laundry nearby. As we said before, to some the small items are more important than the "big" problems.

To help your clients satisfy their individual interests, you may have to consult your local guide, the hotel desk, and/or local directories. This may seem like a lot of extra work, but if, for example, Mr. and Mrs. So-and-So are interested in chamber music and you are able to direct them to a local recital, they will be pleased and will remember your thoughtfulness.

Besides catering to special interests, you should develop a list of items of general interest, such as department store hours, museums, and historic sites in free-day areas. Most big-city and resort hotels offer special sight-seeing tours, and you can tell your group about them and make arrangements if any are interested. However, you should avoid "pushing" your clients into any particular use of their free time.

Age Extremes

Depending on the type and price of the tour, most groups are fairly homogeneous with regard to age. Sometimes, however, you will have someone who is not "in the same mold." For example, grandparents may take a preadolescent grandchild along on a tour. When this happens, you should plan some activities that will be of interest to that person. In this example, the child could be designated as your "assistant" and asked to precount those already on the bus or help count the luggage and find missing clients. Children love being asked to help, and most of them are good at it. Keep such youngsters busy and involved, and the tour will be a happier one.

16. EMERGENCY PROCEDURES

When you are managing a tour, you must be prepared for emergencies. Your clients may get sick or even die. Workers may go out on strike. Businesses may burn down or go bankrupt. Natural disasters may close highways, means of transportation, and other facilities. As the leader of a group, you will have to make quick decisions when such unforeseen situations suddenly arise. Keep calm, use your common sense, and think before you act. Some procedures to aid you in making the right decisions in several emergency situations that might arise are outlined in this section.

Illness of a Client

It is your responsibility, as leader, to see that your clients obtain medical care when needed. You are in charge of your group and should always be on hand to render help and assistance. Hotels in the developed countries have house doctors on call; resort hotels have nursing stations. When a client complains of illness, encourage him to visit the doctor or nurse, and make the appointment for him.

Under no circumstances should you diagnose a client's ailment or give anyone any medicine. For example, if your group is in a mountain resort and a client complains of dizziness, you might feel certain that the altitude is the cause, but there may be another reason. Let the doctor make the diagnosis. You are a tour manager and escort, not a physician. Neither are you a pharmacist, and you will not dispense drugs.

In the more remote parts of the world, doctors are not always available. If one of your clients becomes ill, ask the hotel manager to see if there is a doctor in the house. There may be a doctor among the guests, perhaps even among your own clients. Many physicians do not use their titles when on holiday, but they will care for a fellow tourist who becomes ill. In remote areas, there is usually a flying doctor service for emergencies, and the hotel's management will contact this service when necessary. If the hotel cannot help, try the police. The telephone directory will supply the necessary information.

Because of the great number of North Americans traveling and working in all parts of the world, services have been established to provide lists of English-speaking doctors around the world. Two of the better known ones are: Intermedic, Inc., 777 Third Avenue, New York, N.Y. 10017; and International Association for Medical Assistance to Travelers, 350 Fifth Avenue, New York, N.Y. 10001. Many tour companies subscribe to one or both of these services, so it is wise to ascertain if yours is a member of one of them. In any case, be aware that "unfortunately, in many of the turbulent, developing parts of the world, the lists are all too frequently out of date before they are printed. . . . The physician is likely to be among the elite of any newly independent country, and political changes in the government make the M.D. unavailable either because he has fled or because he has assumed the newer duties of Foreign Minister or President."[15]

In all cases, be familiar with your company's policy for dealing with medical emergencies, particularly when you will be touring in undeveloped areas. Health is a vital factor in touring; be prepared to deal with any health problems that may arise.

A client who is too ill to travel with the tour for a few days may wish to rejoin the group later. Arranging this may be difficult if you are traveling by chartered bus and staying at a resort hotel. If you are able to make such arrangements, inform your company of the change. The usual policy is for the client to pay for his own meals, while separated from the tour and his transportation to rejoin the group (unless you can reticket him). Sometimes he must pay his hotel bill, too. Tell the client that you will inform the company of what he has missed and that he should contact the company upon his return home for a refund.

Advise the company at once if a client must terminate a tour because of illness. If you are traveling by air, the airline will usually issue a separate return ticket for the person who has become ill, provided they are apprised of the situation. If you are traveling by some other means of transportation, or if the airline refuses to issue a special ticket, the client will be responsible for paying his own way. Again, inform him to contact the company and apply for a refund for unused services. The client should always be informed of his rights and told how he can save money and obtain refunds.

If a client's illness requires hospitalization, escort him to the hospital, see that the necessary forms are filled out, and get the name of the attending physician. As soon as the need for hospitalization is apparent, notify your employer by the fastest means available. Most companies give their tour managers a list of night and weekend emergency numbers. Phone, if possible; otherwise, send a telegram or cable. The client's tour reservation form contains a name, address, and number to contact in case of emergency, and the company can make this contact while you are on your way to the hospital. Once the patient is admitted and you have the name of the doctor, perhaps even the diagnosis and prognosis, advise the company office of these facts. The more information the company can supply the next of kin, the better the service to your client.

If you are traveling outside your client's country of citizenship, a call to his consulate or embassy is in order. The people there know how to deal with these emergencies, and you will find them very helpful.

Death of a Client

The illness of a tour member can have an upsetting effect on the rest of the group. A death can cast a pall of gloom that will remain throughout the tour. Your skills as a leader and a diplomat will receive their greatest test if such an unfortunate situation should occur on one of your tours, and you must be prepared for it.

If a member of your group dies, first, notify the local police; then, if the death occurs in a country other than the deceased's home country, advise the appropriate consulate or embassy. If the diplomatic offices are closed, send an "urgent" telegram to the consul or ambassador, giving all of the facts at your disposal. Then advise the tour company of the situation.

Remain with the body until the police have completed their reports and, if necessary, until the consulate has assumed responsibility for the body. Inform the company of the names of the police and consular officials who have taken charge. This information should be detailed, complete, and accurate.

Some companies encourage their managers to keep the death of a client quiet, wherever possible, feeling that such incidents are bad for business. In most cases this is impossible. The excitement, a possible delay in the schedule, the police inquiry—even the "grapevine"—will insure that the group will hear the news. If you handle the situation calmly, diplomatically, and honestly, your attitude will help assure the smooth resumption of the tour.

Forwarding a Group

There are very few situations serious enough to warrant a tour manager's absence from his tour. One such situation might be the hospitalization or death of a client, because it is not always possible to delay the group until all of the formalities have been completed. While even these cases should not become excuses for lengthy absences, there will be times when your absence may have to be prolonged.

If your tour company has a regional office in the area, the person in charge of the office may deploy a local employee as a temporary substitute until you are able to rejoin the group. If the tour is using land transportation, you may be able to complete your work and fly to your destination in time to greet the tour when it arrives. If no substitute escort is available, advise the carrier of the fact. If the group is flying, advise the airline of the situation so one of its service representatives can supervise the move, including customs and immigration, if necessary. Make sure that someone with knowledge and authority is available to help your clients.

Always inform the tour company of your actions, and tell the group who will be looking after them. If you can personally introduce the substitute, so much the better. Your clients are accustomed to your leadership and will not want to be put in other hands or left alone. Airlines, hotels, and other suppliers will generally give the group "red carpet" treatment if they are aware of the circumstances. Again, it cannot be overstressed that your tactful actions will help determine the success of the tour.

Tour Manager's Illness

Illness can be avoided to a certain extent, as we will see in a later section, but your best efforts may not suffice to keep you from getting sick occasionally. Follow the advice you give your clients, and visit the doctor or nursing station at the first sign of illness. If your ailment is serious and you feel you will not be able to continue immediately, advise the company so they can send a replacement. If it is physically impossible for you to continue the tour and your replacement cannot reach the group before they move on, follow the procedure outlined above for forwarding the group. See that there is always someone on hand to help your clients.

Transportation Delays

The public carriers you use have certain legal responsibilities when service is delayed or canceled. These responsibilities vary from carrier to carrier and from country to country. In any case of delay or cancelation of service, approach the transportation company representative with the attitude that you expect the carrier to absorb any costs involved with the delay.

You should expect the carrier to pay for any meal your group may miss and for the use of hotel day rooms, if you are delayed for several hours. If the delay extends to overnight, the carrier should pay for rooms, meals, and transportation from the terminal to the hotel and back.

If you are using land transportation and a delay will either cause you to miss connections or throw the tour itinerary completely off schedule, the carrier will usually fly the group to its next destination. Try to persuade the carrier to pay for refreshments for tour members prior to boarding the plane. Some people take tours that utilize land transportation because they dislike or fear flying, and you will want them to relax. A drink or two sometimes might help them to relax and overcome their discomfort. Use group psychology to bolster any timid members of the tour. Point out that they will be among friends if they fly but will have to travel alone to catch up with the group by land. Occasionally, a client will refuse to fly. Arrange other transportation for him, and assure him that you will be there to meet him at the rejoining point.

As soon as you learn of any delay, assure the tour members that you are taking care of them and inform them of any special consideration that is being shown to them, such as meals or drinks. Make sure they realize that you are in control of the situation.

Common carriers have manuals detailing their procedures in case of delay or cancelation. If the carrier representative does not honor your requests or tells you they cannot be complied with, ask to see the manual. All such discussions, of course, should be held where tour members cannot overhear them.

Since tour companies have special arrangements with individual carriers, many of them on a long-time basis, a switch to another carrier should be initiated by the contracting carrier, not by you. Only in extreme cases—for example, where a carrier insists that the tour sit in the terminal for many hours without meals or other amenities—can you authorize a switch to another carrier, and even in this extreme case you should try to get company permission before you do it. If you are unable to reach anyone in authority before switching carriers, notify the company as soon as possible, explaining the circumstance in detail.

Nonperformance of a Supplier

The tour manager who places his reconfirmation calls faithfully will rarely encounter a failure in service. However, something wholly unforeseen could take place in the time between reconfirmation and arrival to disrupt your arrangements. When such a situation arises, your first act should be to get your group settled somewhere where they can get coffee or other refreshments. Then, try to find an alternate supplier. The management of the organization that was to supply the service may help you, or the tour company or its local office might have standby arrangements. The local tourist office or the police may be of assistance to you also.

When you are faced with this situation, as with all other emergencies, the most important thing you can do is keep cool and use your common sense. Do not alarm the group. Remember that the crisis of today, properly handled, will be the most memorable part of the tour for the group. It will become an excellent topic of conversation later. Do the best you can under the situation, and justify your actions later.

Company Changes En Route

If, when you place your reconfirmation call, the supplier indicates that a service will not be available, notify the tour company at once. If you are familiar with the territory, make suggestions as to possible alternatives.

Some services may deteriorate from one year to the next. Clients' comments and tour managers' reports will bring this to the company's attention, and the office may then change an itinerary while a tour is in progress. When you are advised of such a change, inform the group of the situation and explain that the change is for their benefit. Stress that the change will make the tour more enjoyable. If the change involves skipping a noted attraction, this may require considerable skill on your part. Most travelers, however, can be led to realize that poor service can lessen the enjoyment of any attraction. Your job is to sell the new arrangements to the group and then see to it that the trip is indeed a more enjoyable one.

Expulsion of A Tour Member

On rare occasions you will encounter a client whose behavior is such as to ruin the trip for the other members of the group. Tour managers do not have the right to expel any member of the tour without the consent of the tour company. Many companies, however, have statements in their brochures asserting their right to expel tour members. Some of these statements are phrased in broad paragraphs:

Compatibility of Tour Members: Travel abroad (and sometimes in this country) necessitates being a good-natured realist, as well as a romantic and agreeable acceptance of foreign conditions, accommodations, services and people for what they are and as they exist and not as each of us might prefer them to be. A pleasant tolerance of the different customs, habits and living standards makes for a very enjoyable travel experience. If you are this appreciative traveler, we want you with us because we know you'll be a wonderful companion and that you will have the time of your life. One's health and physical condition are important. If you enjoy a lot of walking and moving about, you will enjoy these tours. Conversely, if you don't enjoy walking and moving about, you won't find these tours agreeable. Be sure to bring comfortable (and not new) walking shoes. If you have a diet problem, these tours are not for you as special preparations of food cannot be assured. These tours are offered to and are restricted to those who are in good physical and mental health without any infirmities, who are understanding and tolerant of the conditions of scheduled group touring abroad and who really enjoy being with a group and participating in group activities. Some travelers, through no fault of their own, find it mentally or physically difficult to enjoy or adjust to the conditions of scheduled group tour activities or to the customs, attitudes and facilities abroad which are naturally different from those accustomed to at home. In all frankness, such travelers should not risk their own happiness and well-being or that of others on the tour by taking one of these Maupintour operated escorted holidays. Maupintour cannot accept or retain such travelers. Our objective is to insure the compatibility, well-being and congeniality of all passengers and the smooth and efficient operation of the tour.[16]

Other tour companies may choose to state their expulsion right in short, blunt statements to the effect that they reserve the right to decline to accept or retain any person as a tour passenger should they deem that such a person's health, mental condition, physical infirmity, or general deportment impede the operation, rights, welfare, or enjoyment of other tour passengers. A refund of unused land tour services is usually the limit of liability.

You should report to the company any member of the tour who is impeding its progress or whose conduct is upsetting other members of the group. Some examples of such behavior, beside the obvious physical ones, are conspicuous alcoholism, public obscenity, and constant profane language. There are laws against this type of behavior all over the world, and a person who persists in engaging in such behavior should quickly be removed from the tour. When such behavior first manifests itself, you should have a private conversation with the offender and try to explain that his conduct is not pleasant. If he refuses to modify his actions, notify your employer at once. To justify your action in seeking his expulsion, make a list of tour members who have been offended by his behavior and a list of his actions, for example, insisting upon drinking from a hip flask after being told by the driver that it was a violation of the ICC rules.

It is always best to report a situation like this by telephone so that action may be taken as quickly as possible. Give your employer all of the information at hand, and ask that the client's trip be terminated. Usually, the tour company will instruct you to present the offending person with a return ticket to his home destination so that he will not be able to seek damages, claiming that he was stranded by the tour.

Advise the group of what happened and of the action you have taken, and ask any member of the tour who was particularly offended by the expelled person to write a statement to be included in your daily report. Such statements will fortify your claim and strengthen the case against the offender.

Expulsion is an extreme measure and should never be considered for tour members who have lesser problems of adjustment or who simply do not fit in with the group. Consider expulsion only when one client's problem(s) gravely disturbs the other members of the group or impedes the operation of the tour so it cannot be conducted in accordance with company policy. Most offenders may be subdued and regulated with tactful and authoritative handling by the tour director.

As tour manager, you must set the leadership role at the very start of the tour. If you are friendly, relaxed, and in full control of situations as they arise, the tour members will develop confidence in your abilities. They will respond to your friendliness by becoming more open with others on the tour and will feel free to relax and enjoy themselves. Identify individual differences, and try to cater to them insofar as you are able. When emergencies arise (and arise they will), know what to do and do it calmly and efficiently. Tour members will offer help and try to contribute to smooth, happy, and pleasant days for all. Your tactful approach to problems as they arise day-in, day-out, will determine the measure of cooperation and assistance you will receive from your clients.

In many ways, including financially, tour management as a work experience fulfills many basic human needs. It is a fine profession whose rewards are plentiful and meaningful when it is properly handled and properly prepared for.

QUESTIONS FOR DISCUSSION

1. A tour begins at the departure site. What steps must the tour manager take to insure a good beginning?
2. What purposes does the informational meeting serve?
3. What techniques should be adopted to avoid problems with "incidental charges?"
4. What information should be imparted on the bus each day? At what times?
5. Explain the statement, "A good tour manager knows when to talk and when to shut up."
6. What techniques may an escort use to break up a long, dull ride?
7. What types of meals are offered on tour? How do they differ from each other?
8. Outline the procedures to follow when a client becomes seriously ill.
9. What steps must the tour manager follow upon the death of a client?
10. Expulsion of a client is a very serious matter. How should the manager prepare for such an eventuality?
11. What are some ways in which a tour manager can meet the individual needs of his clients?

NOTES

1. Four Winds Tours, *General Tour Manager's Manual,* 1975, p. 4.
2. Village Luggage, Inc., Rockville Centre, N.Y.

3. British Airways Publication 8727, "New Free Baggage Allowance for Transatlantic Travel," p. 2.
4. Greyhound World Tours, *Escort's Training Manual*, 1975, p. 3.
5. See Olsen Tours, *Olsen Europe, 1975*, p. 124; and/or Trans World Airlines, *TWA Getaway Europe, 1975*, p. 142.
6. For a complete account of bus designs, see "Motorcoach Tours Come of Age," Perspective section of *Travel Weekly*, Sept. 2, 1976, pp. 9-17.
7. Amexco, *American Express to Europe: The Escorted Way*, 1976, p. 7.
8. "Diary of a Tour Escort," *Travel Weekly*, Aug. 1, 1974, p. 23.
9. Donald Lundberg, *The Tourist Business*, 3rd ed. (Boston: CBI Publishing Company, Inc., 1972), p. 146.
10. Greyhound World Tours, Inc., *Escort's Training Manual*, 1975, p. 2.
11. Ibid., pp. 1-2.
12. "Diary of a Tour Escort," *Travel Weekly*, Aug. 1, 1974, p. 23.
13. *Travel Weekly*, Nov. 27, 1975, p. 8D.
14. Conversation with the author, Canadian Thanksgiving, 1975.
15. Kevin M. Cahill, *Medical Advice for the Traveler* (New York: Holt, Rinehart and Winston, New York, 1970), p. 65.
16. Maupintours, *Europe, 1975*, p. 38.

PART 5

The Personal Side of Tour Management

Our escorts are a good deal more than the title implies. They are mature, resourceful, and travel-wise—carefully chosen from hundreds of applicants for their background and training. . . . They take care of all the details so that you are completely free to have a wonderful time. Forget about schedules and connections and transfers and baggage . . . Your escorts are informative. They are good company too.
Four Winds brochure

17. PERSONAL PRO'S AND CON'S

Tour management means hard work and long hours. It is not easy to please everybody; yet service is the name of the profession. The tour manager is away from home much of the time, lives out of a suitcase, and is always "on stage." Yet, those men and women whose profession it is love it. Laurance Shaffer and Edward Shoben state, "Another invaluable factor in mental health is constructive work. . . . work has its best hygienic value when it is characterized by freedom and success. . . . the sense and satisfaction that comes from work well done can be one of the strongest integrating experiences in your life."[1] Newspapermen used to say that printers' ink got in their blood, meaning that once they had experienced the excitement of their occupation they would not be happy doing anything else. This is also true of tour management. On tour, you are free of the office; you are the boss. To your clients, you are a combination of many pleasant things: teacher, guide, entertainer, friend.

Travel itself is one of the rewards of tour management. Lundberg points out that "travel for travel's sake is a self-perpetuating phenomenon. . . . much of travel has no real excuse other than the pleasure of travel."[2] While escorting a tour, you are always meeting new people, seeing new places, and facing new challenges, all the while learning new facts. In addition, there is the ego-enhancing feeling of always being needed.

The Tour Manager's Spouse

One question consistently asked of married tour escorts is, "How can your wife/husband stand you being away so much?" The true answer is, "It is not easy." While it is true that in some cases either the career or the marriage ended, it is possible to have both a successful career and a happy marriage. As with any business or profession, however, the patience and understanding of both parties is required.

Tour managers visit some of the most interesting and exciting places in the world. On-the-job experiences and knowledge gained broaden the intellect, and extend one's acculturation. These are qualities that could enliven and enhance any marriage. Small gifts and souvenirs can make far-away places come alive for the spouse left at home. In addition to the regular periodic exception (duty free allowance), the traveler may mail home each day, free of duty charges, gifts valued at up to $10 each to a residence in U.S.A., or up to $15 each to a residence in Canada. Such gifts must be clearly marked "unsolicited gift."

It must be realized that what a tour manager does for a living is what most people do for a vacation. Conversely, a tour manager on vacation might want to spend much of his time in what a spouse might consider a dull routine. For example, home cooking is a luxury when you have been out on a tour for thirty-eight days, but your spouse may be looking forward to dining out occasionally while you are at home. The solution to this problem, as to any other in a working marriage, is to compromise or "make a deal." You must organize an arrangement favorable to both; for example, some nights dine in, and the others dine out.

Many tour companies have rules against their tour managers "bringing someone along" on a tour, and for very good reasons. People have paid for the full attention of the escort. However, married managers who have worked for the company for a period of time can usually get permission for their mates to join a special tour.

Your spouse should not join you until after you have established yourself as tour leader, preferably about the time the group has a free day. A day or two before this occurs, announce that your spouse will be joining you and that he/she may be with the group for a few days. On the day that he or she arrives, make yourself visible in the hotel lobby, and introduce your mate to as many of the clientele as you meet. At the same time, ask them if they are having a good time and if everything is going well.

As the tour continues, follow this rule: While you are working, your spouse is not on tour. If you are careful about this, no tour member can say that you slighted him or her. You will know you are handling the situation well when one of the group says, "Will you please go back and sit with your husband/wife for a while?"

Your spouse should always leave prior to the last days of the tour. At the farewell dinner, you can report his or her safe arrival home and express your gratitude to the group for their kindness to your spouse.

While a few companies may occasionally pay the air fare for the spouse of one of their long-time tour managers, it is more usual for you to pay for it. If you have been working the same tour for a while, advise the hotels that your spouse will be joining you; usually, they will give you a larger room and include your spouse in any tour-connected meals.

Never forget that yours is considered a glamourous job. Having your mate join you once in a while gives you an opportunity to demonstrate that it is also hard work. Your spouse will also share some of the sights you see and the people you meet, and this sharing will reinforce the marriage bond.

18. THE FINANCIAL SIDE OF TOUR MANAGEMENT

There are many financial considerations in tour management. To begin with, you are entrusted with a sizable amount of company money with which to run the tour. It is imperative that you safeguard these funds and keep accurate records of their expenditure. The records you keep will also determine whether refunds are due to any of your tour members. In addition to company money, you will be carrying your subsistence allowance and, in some cases, part of your salary. You must keep these funds separate from company money so that you can make an accurate accounting of the latter.

Salary

The tour manager's basic salary is computed and paid in different ways by different companies. Some pay an hourly rate (usually the minimum hourly rate allowed by the Labor Department where the company has its headquarters), while most pay a per diem rate and the occasional one pays on a per tour basis. While no North American survey of tour managers' salaries has been published, a British study in 1974 showed that "the best guides [tour managers] earn about $25.00 per day."[3]

In the spring of 1977, the United States region of the International Association of Tour Managers (IATM) conducted its own survey. The results showed that for that year a professional tour manager averaged $40.00 per day for overseas tours, somewhat less for domestic tours. The highest salary shown in the survey, for multilingual tour managers managing a tour of mixed foreign nationals, was $50.00 per day.[4] All of the companies surveyed paid one half of the salary at the beginning of the tour and the remainder upon completion. For domestic tours, the average salary was about $27.00 per day.

Subsistence

In addition to your basic salary, you are given a sum of money to cover meals not included in the itinerary, laundry, tips, and other incidental expenses. Sometimes this amount is issued as a separate check, and sometimes it is included in the tour expense account.

Most companies allow a standard amount for meals and laundry charges, and this is not accountable. This means that it is yours to spend as you choose. With proper handling, this fund is usually sufficient to cover all of your personal expenses while on tour, leaving your salary as untouched savings.

Gratuities

Almost every tour company includes a statement in its brochure concerning gratuities to tour managers. This one is typical: "Gratuities: All gratuities to hotel staff and guides for normal tour services are included. The customary end-of-tour gratuity to the Tour Manager is not included, and is optional at the discretion of the tour member."[5]

It will be to your advantage to set a pattern of individual tipping early in the tour. As we suggested earlier, you should encourage your clients to individually tip local guides and other personnel who give service beyond what would ordinarily be expected. Tell them that individual gratuities, given with a word of encouragement and thanks, always mean more than an anonymous group gift. If the group has become accustomed to individual tipping, they will handle your gratuity the same way.

Other Income

As we mentioned earlier, a manager is occasionally able to arrange side tours for people with special interests, and he usually receives a commission from the local sight-seeing company with whom these arrangements are made. On other occasions, some of the people on your tour may want to see the "night life" of a large city. Arranging a nightclub tour with the hotel's sight-seeing desk is an excellent source of "commission money."

Occasionally, a store manager will give a small present or a discount to a tour manager if the tour patronizes his store, as will a restaurant manager for recommending his restaurant for a meal that is not included in the tour itinerary. These transactions should never be witnessed by the tour clientele. No client should ever feel that he was forced to visit a shop or eat in a restaurant or pressured by you to spend his time and/or money in any manner other than his own choosing.

19. HANDLING COMPANY MONEY

At the beginning of each tour, you will receive a check to cover all the nonvouchered expenses of the tour. This is the money you must account for in your expense report. This report should always be kept as up to the minute as possible. Record as you spend, and balance your money every evening.

The Expense Fund

The expense fund should be converted into travelers' checks as soon as you receive it. Keep a record of the numbers of the checks apart from the book of checks itself. Each evening, after you have balanced your accounts, the checks and cash should be put in the safe-deposit box or other suitable place provided by the innkeeper.

Know what is allowed for each service that must be paid for out of the expense account; some companies list allowances on the expense account form, while others put them in the escorts' manual.

The Emergency Fund

The amount of money in the expense-fund check is usually larger than the estimated nonvouchered expenses, to allow for emergencies. This additional amount varies from company to company. It is usually based on the number of people on the tour or the length of the tour. The emergency fund is to be used when there is a change in the itinerary, whether initiated by the company or due to nonperformance by a supplier. Most experienced escorts carry blank vouchers to cover such emergencies and use the cash only when a voucher is refused. When you must use the cash, notify the company at once and have it replaced.

Use this fund if, for example, a client needs money in a medical emergency. Most companies have a policy about advancing money to a client in such cases; know your company's policy before you act.

Tour Manager's Credit Cards

You should always carry your own credit cards on tour with you. You should have (1) an internationally recognized air travel card such as "En Route" (Air Canada) or "Getaway" (Trans World Airlines) and (2) an international bank card like Master Charge or Visa. Besides being personally convenient, these cards will come in handy when you do not have sufficient cash in the emergency fund.

Remember that when you use your own credit card you are personally liable for the bill. Therefore, you should always pre-clear its use with your employer prior to the start of the tour. Have this clearance in writing, if possible. When you must use your own card for company business, have the supplier of the service endorse the bill as follows: "For services rendered to Tour # ___ of ___ Tour Company." Since most credit cards have limits on the amount of credit that may be extended, try to have your employer issue a check to the credit card company immediately upon receipt of your copy (the tissue copy) of the transaction.

Client Refunds

If a client requests a service that is not included in the tour, he must pay for the service directly. However, when a client does not get something to which he is entitled—for example, if he is down-graded or terminates early—he is entitled to some sort of refund.

Since tour costs are based upon wholesale rates, you should never tell a client that he is entitled to any specific amount. Advise him to write to the company explaining what was missed. Tell him that you, too, will give the company this information (it should be on your report of missed services) and that he will hear from the company as to the amount of refund.

20. THE TOUR MANAGER'S HEALTH

While changes in climate, water, or food may adversely affect some of your clients on any particular tour, you, the tour manager, are expected to be immune to these hazards of travel. The profession requires all who enter it to be in excellent health and to know how to stay that way.

It is possible for you to go from winter to summer several times in one season if your tours run between the northern and southern hemispheres. Even if you stay in North America, your tours may take you from the cool Canadian north to the tropical climate of Yucatán.

Besides encountering climatic changes, you may be traveling through parts of the world where "exotic" diseases are part of everyday life. The motto, "An ounce of prevention is worth a pound of cure" (or, to follow the metric system, "28.35 grams of prevention is worth 453.4 grams of cure"), is the watchword of all good tour managers.

Inoculations

Besides a current passport, you should have in your possession an International Certificate of Vaccination form, which is issued by your local public health service, as approved by the World Health Organization of the United Nations. If you expect to lead tours outside North America and western Europe, you should be inoculated against smallpox, tetanus, polio, typhoid, and yellow fever. An inoculation against cholera is recommended for Asian travel. All these inoculations should not be taken at one time, and some require multiple shots to provide immunity. One of the best sources of information on this and other topics related to health is *Medical Advice for the Traveler* by Dr. Kevin Cahill.[6] This seventy-nine-page book should be part of your library and is compact enough to be part of your luggage. Once you have received these inoculations, keep them up to date by getting booster shots when necessary.

Medical Kit

Although common carriers around the world carry first-aid kits, you, as a tour manager, should carry some medication and supplies of your own. Besides such ordinary items as bandages, cotton, sunburn lotion and aspirin, Cahill suggests that all travelers carry an antihistamine (like Chlortrimeton or Benedryl), pills for motion sickness, paregoric, an antibiotic (like tetracycline), and sleeping pills. For the tropical traveler, he adds an analgesic (like codeine), salt tablets, insect repellents, disposable needles, and an antimalarial.[7] Many of these items are available only by prescription, so you should request such prescriptions from your physician at the time of your annual physical examination.

Annual Physical Examination

All tour managers should undergo a complete annual physical checkup by a physician. The work of a manager is physically demanding and requires that one always be in tip-top shape.

If the same physician is used every year, he will be able to maintain complete records and can schedule chest X-rays and EKGs when necessary. He will know your line of work and can write the necessary prescriptions for your medical kit and keep your inoculations up to date.

21. MAIL AND MESSAGES

Before going on a tour, you will receive a hotel list similar to that given to all of the clients. This will give your family a place to contact you in an emergency. However, hotels are not the best places to plan to receive your mail.

If your company has offices in any of the cities you will visit, you might arrange to have your mail sent there. Or, if you are working the same tour on a regular basis, you might rent a post-office box where the midtour free time is scheduled. Overseas, if you have free time in a city where a consulate is located, you might arrange to have your mail sent in care of the consulate.

If none of the above is possible, or if you are not on a regular tour basis, select only hotels where you will be staying two or more nights as mailing addresses. You can then get to know the clerk who handles the mail and ask him to recheck if he says there is none for you. Hotels hold mail by guests' names, by tour names, and sometimes even by tour numbers and it takes time to check all three. Any mail addressed to you at a hotel should include your name, the title "Tour Manager," the tour company name, and the number of the tour as well as the arrival date.

QUESTIONS FOR DISCUSSION

1. What are the major components of the total earnings of a tour manager?
2. The tour manager must possess excellent health and maintain it. What steps can he take to insure his own good health?
3. Why is the inclusion in a tour of the tour manager's spouse a sensitive matter? How can this be handled without clients feeling slighted?
4. Discuss how the tour manager can safeguard the company money entrusted to him.

NOTES

1. Laurance F. Shaffer and Edward J. Shoben, Jr., *The Psychology of Adjustment* (Boston: Houghton Mifflin Co., 1956), pp. 588-589.

2. Donald Lundberg, *The Tourist Business,* 3rd ed. (Boston: CBI Publishing Company, Inc., 1972), p. 141.
3. *Travel Weekly,* Aug. 1, 1974, p. 23.
4. Pierre J. Bouchier, "Report of Tour Managers' Salaries," given at meeting of U.S. Region, IATM, New York, Mar. 1, 1977.
5. Travcoa Tours, *Orient and South Pacific, 1976,* p. 40.
6. Kevin M. Cahill, *Medical Advice for the Traveler,* (New York: Holt, Rinehart and Winston, 1970).
7. Ibid., p. 34.

PART 6

Problems in the Profession

One should know that our daily salaries are terribly low in proportion to all the responsibilities we assume and the amount of knowledge that is expected of us. Many tour managers work fewer than 180 days a year. Our periods of unemployment are uninsured.
Le Monde

22. CURRENT PROBLEMS

As in any job or profession, there are in tour management areas that need improvement, conditions that need study, and benefits that should be added to the tour manager's compensation.

In the mid-1970s, *Le Monde,* the Paris newspaper, began publishing articles about the difficulties encountered by tour guides. In an article entitled, "L'ancienneté au salaire d'un débutant" (seniority and beginning wages), Yvette Mir pointed out one major problem when she stated:

> Exception faite des satisfactions personelles qu'éprouvent les guides-interprètes après avoir rempli leur rôle auprès des visiteurs étrangers, que peuvent-ils espérer en contrepartie de ces difficultés? Presque rien: aucune ancienneté, le salaire d'un débutant étant exactement le même que celui d'un guide chevronné ayant quinze années d'expérience.[1]

Few tour companies give credit for prior experience. Any per-diem increase from year to year is the result of inflation. Thus, if this is your fifth year with Company X and you have a total of fifteen years' experience, you will get the same daily rate as another person working his first tour for Company X.

Another problem is the lack of insurance protection provided by the companies for tour managers. If an accident should occur, the company position is that the insurance coverage of the carrier, hotel, or other supplier will take care of the tour manager. As an independent contractor, the manager is not covered by the group policy that covers the company's full-time employees, and hospitalization insurance on an individual basis is quite expensive.

The United States region of the International Association of Tour Managers is presently studying, first, the possibility of a group insurance policy for its members and, second, a drive to have the employers purchase insurance to cover tour managers while they are on tour.

The fact that tour managers are independent contractors brings up another problem, their inability to claim unemployment insurance in some jurisdictions. Labor departments require continuous employment by one employer for a set period of time as a condition for the collection of this type of insurance. There are times of the year when tourism is slow, and there are periods of recession (as in the mid-1970s) when there is a slowdown in the normal busy periods. The recognition of the profession of tour manager by governments—with all of its special situations—is a major aim of the IATM. Professional recognition, including national licensing, has been achieved in some countries.

With the recent growth in the number of tour companies (see Friedheim, "Anyone Can Be a Tour Operator,"[2] or Goodwin, "Selecting a Tour Wholesaler"[3]) we are again seeing the hiring of unqualified people to act as tour escorts. This is a growing concern. In an unsigned article in *Le Monde,* one disgusted tour manager wrote:

> Comédiens, représentants, étudiants, ex-stewards et hôtesses, infirmiers, assistantes dentaires, retraités, personnels de l'éducation nationale—y compris des professeurs!—pendant les périodes de congés scolaires viennent ainsi occuper des emplois de courriers, alors que ces derniers restent inscrits comme demandeurs d'emploi. Nous tenons à insister sur le fait que dans la plupart des cas ces personnes ignorent tout des responsabilités qu'elles devrent assurer comme des connaissances qu'elles devraient posséder, et, de ce fait, lésent gravement les intérêts de la clientèle qu'elles se voient confier.[4]

The article goes on to point out the shortsightedness of hiring such people in the name of economy. In the long run they lose both money and clientele. According to the author, the tour manager must supervise the completion of the contracts, handle large sums of money, make instant decisions based upon knowledge and experience, and at the same time entertain and instruct the group. To do the latter, he must have a knowledge of geography, history, economics, and the customs of each region, as well as its art, religion, and life-styles. To this indispensable knowledge, he must add a sense of organization and the ability to direct a group made up of very different people. The International Association of Tour Managers is presently campaigning to advise companies of the problems they will encounter by using untrained people as escorts.

Another major problem facing the tour manager is the cancelation of a tour by a company. Tour managers are usually contracted a few months before a tour is scheduled to depart. If for some reason (other than your own serious personal illness) you do not work the tour, you will probably never be hired by that operator again. But if for some reason the operator cancels the tour, he can notify you at the last minute and you are left without work. Usually, it is then too late to get work with another tour company for that period of time. The U.S. region of the IATM is beginning a study to see if a cancelation clause can be written into tour management contracts. At present, the companies are opposed to such an idea.

23. THE INTERNATIONAL ASSOCIATION
OF TOUR MANAGERS

Just as every profession has its organization to deal with problems within the field and lobby for governmental action as well as to share expertise, tour management has the International Association of Tour Managers. The purposes of IATM are:

1. To represent Tour Managers at international congresses of travel organizations
2. To voice the opinion of Tour Managers through trade meetings and the travel press
3. To give Tour Managers contacts in all parts of the world[5]

Each quarter the IATM publishes a newsletter which keeps the membership abreast of developments in the field of tour management around the world. Members also receive a directory, updated annually, of all members. This directory serves as an excellent resource when a member runs into problems in an unfamiliar place. All IATM members are pledged to come to each other's aid by suggesting alternate accommodations, seeking local help, and so on.

Once each year an international congress is held, where problems are discussed and remedial actions initiated.

The association also maintains a "job bank" in each country to inform members of companies seeking tour managers. In addition, the job bank and the regional organization screen tour operators and agents who are running tours.

To be considered for membership, one must have had two years' experience escorting tours and a strong recommendation from one's employer(s). In addition, the applicant must be sponsored and seconded by two IATM members.

Further information may be obtained by contacting: The International Association of Tour Managers, 397 Walworth Road, London SE17, England; or, Dr. Patrick J. Curran, Box 506, Jasper, Alberta, Canada TOE-IEO.

Tours are people, and people are human. Although every attempt has been made in this book to cover the usual situations encountered in leading escorted tours, when dealing with people it is impossible to anticipate everything.

What do you do about the husband and wife who have had a fight and will not speak to each other except through you? What if a bus blows two tires in the middle of nowhere? You will encounter many situations that call for cool thinking, diplomacy, psychology, some humor. Handling them successfully is what makes you a tour manager.

Unfortunately, some clients will not be satisfied, no matter what you do. Accept this as part of your job, because you cannot be all things to all people. You will make mistakes; admit them, and try to rectify them. You will experience a sense of satisfaction that few jobs can offer when, at the farewell dinner at the end of the tour, people tell you what a great job you did. You should not be surprised when you hear, years later, from people who still remember some particular incident or some kindness that you showed them. This makes all the preparation, aggravation, and work worthwhile.

QUESTIONS FOR DISCUSSION

1. What are some of the current problems facing the profession? How might some of these problems be resolved?
2. What is the IATM? What purposes does it serve?

NOTES

1. *Le Monde,* Jan. 19, 1977, p. 18. Translation (by Barbara Gallagher): "Other than personal satisfaction which tour managers experience on the job, what can they hope for to counteract the disadvantages? Almost nothing—no seniority. The wages of a beginner are exactly the same as a highly knowledgeable guide with fifteen years' experience."
2. Eric Friedheim, "Anyone Can Be a Tour Operator," *The Travel Agent,* Feb. 7, 1977, p. 82.
3. Nadine Goodwin, "Selecting a Tour Wholesaler," *Travel Weekly,* Perspective, Oct. 30, 1975, pp. 61–64A.
4. *Le Monde,* loc. cit. "Comedians, representatives, students, ex-stewards, hostesses, nurses, dental assistants, retirees, employees in the state education system—even professors included here—during vacation periods take

up the jobs of tour managers, while the latter seek work. We must insist upon the fact that in the majority of cases these people ignore all the responsibilities they should assume as well as the knowledge which they should possess."

5. International Association of Tour Managers, *Advantages of Belonging to IATM* (London, 1974), p. 2.

Glossary

A la carte dining   Diner's choice of anything offered on the menu.

Courier   The European term for a tour escort.

Customs   The procedure at an international border or port of entry in which the entrant declares what he is bringing into that nation.

Deluxe   The best available in accommodations, food, and so on, provided with special elegance and luxury.

Downgrading   Giving a person something of lesser value than he expected or contracted for.

Duty-free shop   A store located in an international airport or at a port of exit that sells goods free of taxes to travelers going into another country.

Economy   A step down from first class, moderate in quality, comfort, and price (sometimes called tourist class).

Escort   An employee of a tour company or agency who accompanies a tour to see that all of the services are provided. This employee does not meet the qualifications of a tour manager.

Escorted tour   A tour accompanied by an employee of the company or agency that arranged the tour, who handles the details of the tour.

Expulsion   The removal of a client from a tour because his actions or behavior are offensive or detrimental to the other members of the tour.

First class The best quality but without the elegance or luxury associated with the deluxe classification. In air travel, first class is the highest classification.

Foreign exchange The conversion of the money of one nation into that of another.

Group tour A number of people traveling together and following an itinerary set up by a tour company or travel agency.

Guide A person employed to conduct sight-seeing at a particular place or city.

The International Association of Tour Managers (IATM) A worldwide association of professional tour managers, head-quartered in London, that looks after the interests and investigates the problems of its members.

Immigration The procedure followed at an international border or port of entry to gain admission to a nation.

Incidental charges Charges for personal services, such as laundry, telephone, and so on, that are not part of the tour price and that the client has billed to his hotel room.

Inclusive tour A tour that includes most meals and the sight-seeing charges in each area visited.

Independent contractor One who is hired to do a particular job for a set period of time.

Independent tour A tour that does not include the services of an escort or tour manager.

Individual tour A tour planned for one individual or a small group, such as a family.

Information meeting A meeting of all tour members held shortly after the beginning of a tour to review what is included in the tour, the method of check signing, tipping, incidental charges, and so on.

No shows People holding paid and confirmed tickets for a tour or other transportation who do not arrive by departure time.

Options Activities other than those included in the tour price (e.g., a night club tour) that may be elected by a tour member upon payment of an additional fee, usually at the time of the activity.

Passport   A booklet issued by a nation to its citizens, permitting them to travel abroad.

Per diem   Money paid on a daily basis, as salary or for expenses.

Seat rotation   An organized scheme by which tour members regularly change seats on a tour bus so that each person has an opportunity to sit up front as well as over the wheels.

Set menu dining   A menu preselected by the tour operator, offering few if any choices. If choices are offered, they are in the main course only.

Share   A person traveling alone who is willing to room with another single traveler to avoid paying the extra charge for a single supplement.

Single supplement   An additional charge levied on a traveler for single occupancy of a hotel room.

Steering   The strong recommendation of certain stores and restaurants by a sight-seeing guide, escort, or tour manager.

Stiffing   The deliberate withholding of a gratuity when one is expected and deserved.

Subsistence   Money paid for living expenses while one is on the road. It includes money for meals and hotels not included in the tour as well as for laundry and gratuities.

Surcharge   An additional amount of money that a client must pay when he voluntarily chooses better accommodations than those offered in the tour package.

Table d'hôte dining   A meal of prearranged choices, with choices within each course, the price of which is set regardless of the choices made. This type of menu is usually offered to guests of hotels and resorts.

Tour   A trip planned by a tour company or travel agent, for which the client pays in advance. It may include transportation, accommodations, and sometimes sight-seeing and meals.

Tour director   A synonym for escort.

Tour manager   A trained and experienced person of demonstrated ability who accompanies a tour, sees that all services are provided, and gives the clients the historical and cultural background of the areas visited.

Tour menu dining A menu preselected by a tour operator, which offers limited choices in each course.

Tourist card A document issued to tourists (particularly by Latin American nations) in place of a visa or passport.

Upgrading Giving a person something better than they expected or contracted for.

Visa Permission by a nation for a foreigner to enter it, usually in the form of a stamp affixed to the visitor's passport.

Voucher A signed statement of services rendered, authorizing payment for such services.

Index

About the Author

Patrick J.T. Curran grew up in Lansdowne, Ontario. Having earned his B.A. and M.A. at Fordham University, the author went on to earn his M.Ed. at Teachers College, Columbia University, and his Ph.D. at North Texas State University. Dr. Curran entered the travel industry as a tour escort for Casser Tours while a student at Columbia University. Throughout the past seventeen years he has been employed by or has served as a consultant to several of the largest tour operators in North America. In February 1978 he joined the faculty of Adelphi University in Garden City, New York as a Professor of Tourism. When not on Long Island, the author resides in Jasper, Alberta.

Samuel I. Porrath wrote the foreword to this volume. Educator, lecturer, and world traveler, Dr. Porrath is the founder and current chairman of the Institute of Transportation, Travel and Tourism (TTT) at Niagara University, Niagara Falls, New York. It is the first institution of higher learning to have created an academic curriculum toward a baccalaureate degree in the multifaceted area of the TTT industries. Since is founding in July 1968, the Institute has graduated over 500 men and women. Its present enrollment is in excess of 400 students.